TAKE A WALK, *Louisville!*

NATURE EXCURSIONS IN AND AROUND LOUISVILLE, KENTUCKY

By Lucynda Koesters

Photography by Willi H. Koesters

Also by Lucynda and Willi Koesters
Take A Hike, Louisville!

Approval by the Commonwealth of Kentucky Transportation Cabinet
of the reproduction of a portion of the Kentucky Official Highway map
on pages 16-17 should in no way be construed as promotion
of any product advertised herein.

ISBN 978-1-941953-14-3
Printed in the United States of America

Photography by Willi H. Koesters

Front and back cover photography was taken at
Perrin Family Park in Jeffersonville, Indiana (Clark County)

Book design by Scott Stortz

Published by:

Butler Books
P.O. Box 7311
Louisville, KY 40257
(502) 897–9393
Fax (502) 897–9797
www.butlerbooks.com

For

Carol Kaufmann,

Bird lover, pet lover, nature cheerleader,
mentor, and dear friend

Special Thanks

Tavia Cathcart Brown and Carol Butler,
two of the loveliest, most supportive and
cheerful ladies I've ever known.

Your optimism inspires me.

Thank you!

TABLE OF CONTENTS

THE PARKLANDS OF FLOYDS FORK

ADDITIONAL WALKING PATHS FROM
TAKE A HIKE, LOUISVILLE!

INTRODUCTION

In our first book, *Take A Hike Louisville!*, we asked the question, "Why should one want to take a hike?" We pointed out that no matter what age or stage of life you are in, everyone can enjoy substantial mental and physical benefits from getting out and enjoying nature. We highlighted some facts from Richard Louv's wonderful book, *Last Child in the Woods*, in which he discussed "nature-deficit disorder," or the human costs of alienation from nature: diminished use of the senses, attention difficulties, and higher rates of physical and emotional illnesses. While this disorder is often attributed to children, people of all ages can suffer from a lack of connections to the natural world. Mr. Louv cites a body of evidence indicating that direct exposure to nature is essential for physical and mental health, especially in increasing cognitive capacity and resistance to stress and anxiety.

Over the six years since our first book was published, my husband and I have "aged gracefully," or at least that is what we optimistically consider has happened. We find that hikes once considered easy have now become moderate, and strenuous hiking is something we simply do not feel too motivated to take on any longer. However, we still have our love of the outdoors and make getting out in nature a priority. We certainly do feel the effects of our "graceful aging" on our bones and joints, and have each fought minor battles with arthritis and injuries.

During this period, I experienced a career transition that led me to working with senior citizens, most recently as a meals-on-wheels and senior center director for LifeSpan Resources, an Area Agency on Aging in southern Indiana. This work raised my awareness even more as to the issues surrounding the health and wellness of our aging population.

In spite of my own slowdown in terms of hiking capacity, and in what I observe working with seniors, I still have the heart and mind to get outdoors and enjoy the many wonderful benefits of nature, and I am inspired at even greater levels to share the ways and means to accomplish this with my elderly clientele.

A wonderful evidence-based program offered at LifeSpan is called *Walk with Ease©*, developed by the Arthritis Foundation. While I am aware of the benefits of nature on one's mental and physical health, this program proves just how beneficial simply walking is, especially for those older people with arthritis.

According to the Arthritis Foundation, walking can have the following benefits on one's health:

- Strengthens the heart and lungs
- Nourishes joints
- Builds bones
- Fights osteoporosis
- Burns calories
- Controls weight
- Reduces stress
- Improves mood
- Boosts energy

With all of these physical benefits of simply walking a little each day, combined with the mental and spiritual boosts you will get just by being in nature, we aim to present a walking guide to Louisville-area nature paths and "gentle" hikes.

In "*Take A Walk, Louisville!*, we have scoped out more than 25 new walks for you to explore and enjoy. Most have paved walkways with gentle inclines. A few are hiking trails or grassy paths. Once again, we have found that an abundance of wonderful and easily accessible nature areas exist right here in our own Louisville backyard.

Walking benefits your body and spirit. It is inexpensive, convenient, and enjoyable and coupled with the fresh air and scenery of nature, mood elevating as well. Walking puts less stress on older bodies than most other forms of exercise, but offers many of the same health-boosting benefits.

So what are you waiting for?

It's time to get out and take a simple walk in the woods. Take your time and use your senses. Listen to birdsong, wind rustling through treetop leaves and water lapping a river shore. View golden sunsets, russet leaves fluttering in the fall, clear blue skies with cotton puff clouds drifting by. Touch cool soft moss on rocks or splashing water off a stream ledge. Breathe in the aroma of the woods: earthy peat and damp leaves, meadow honeysuckle or wild dill. Savor it all slowly and gently.

There are many walking paths, nature trails, and meadow walkways to enjoy right here in the Louisville area. As we found in our first book, the variety of nature experiences in the Louisville area will astound you. And since that time, a wonderful new nature resource, the Parklands of Floyds Fork, has opened up a new bounty of parklands, trails, streams, ponds, wetlands, meadows, walking paths, and more to explore.

A FEW HEALTH CONSIDERATIONS BEFORE YOU BEGIN

If you have been sedentary for a while or have any concerning health conditions, please talk to your health care provider before starting a walking program. The American Physical Therapy Association asks *Walk with Ease©* participants to consider these questions before embarking:

- Do you have heart trouble?
- Do you have chest pain on your left side (neck, shoulder, arm)?
- Do you get breathless with physical activity?
- Do you feel faint often or have dizzy spells?
- Do you have high blood pressure?

- Do you have bone or joint problems that could worsen with physical activity?
- Are you older than 50 and not physically active?

If you can answer NO to all of these questions, you can likely take on a moderate walking program.

If you answered YES to any of them, we recommend you check with your health care provider before beginning.

When walking, be alert for physical signs of danger: severe pain, pressure in your chest, nausea, difficulty breathing, dizziness, severe trembling or light-headedness. If you experience any of these, stop and call 911 from your mobile phone.

Signs of overdoing it include a very red face or a very pale one, sweating heavily, joint pain lasting more than two hours after walking, or feeling extremely tired. If you have any of these symptoms, please slow down; you are overdoing it. If you are just beginning a walking program, please take it easy and start slowly. That really is what this book is all about—ease of use, ease of walking, ease of access to nature, and most of all, a pleasant afternoon.

One last thing this book is about: ice cream. Yes, you read that right—ice cream. In my work with seniors, I realize that ice cream is one of life's greatest pleasures—not just for senior citizens, but for everyone. Who doesn't just love a cold frosty treat on a warm afternoon?

We ended all of our walks in this book with a stop for an ice cream treat. Not only did the two "old folks" love it, but so did any other walkers who came along with us, especially our preteen daughter who is our constant walking and hiking companion. In fact, she would remind me as we were walking along our trail not to forget to google the nearest ice cream shop.

We found a good spot for a cool treat very easy to find after our walks. There was always either a local ice creamery, a frozen yogurt shop, Starbucks, Dairy Queen, or McDonald's close by. I am very cognizant as a meals-on-wheels and senior nutrition director, and for myself as well, of the massive problem we have in our country and in our own community, with diabetes. I am always watching my sugar intake. However, I found it very easy on these excursions to select a low-sugar option such as sugar-free, low-fat frozen yogurt, sugar-free Dilly Bar, fruit and protein smoothies, or plain iced coffee when enjoying our ice cream stop. I never felt deprived, as my husband is careful with his diet as well. Our treat stop added so much more to our outings than just a chance to gobble something sweet: more time together before heading back to our busy and stressful workaday lives.

We wrote this book over the course of a year, rarely missing a weekend walk. Except for the very cold polar vortex winter days, we were out in all weather conditions and immensely enjoyed watching the seasons change.

Being in nature never fails to revive the soul. I learned to rely on my weekend walks for stress relief and looked forward to the rejuvenation and mental health boost I knew they would provide. My great love of being outdoors will permeate my write-ups at times in this book—I hope you don't mind. I hope you enjoy walking along these beautiful paths and trails with our family for a bit before you head out on your own. I am extremely grateful for my health and the physical ability to get outside in nature—even as I glide slowly through my middle-age years.

So, now it's your turn to embrace nature, get outside, and Take A Walk!

HOW TO USE THIS BOOK

Each section in this book features a short walk with a nature feature. You may wind through woodlands, wetlands, or meadowlands, or along streams, lakes, or rivers. You'll find creeks, boulders, old-growth forests, dense brush, wildflowers, fishing ponds, and more. Our goal is to get you into nature in the easiest and most accessible way possible. Most walks in this book are no longer than a mile or two. Many are paved and handicap accessible. A few are hiking trails or grassy walkways. We will tell you where to park, where to find the trail, and how to make your way back to your car. We have also described the area's amenities, such as picnic shelters and restroom facilities.

WHAT TO PACK AHEAD OF TIME

We suggest packing a few items ahead of time and keeping a "walking package" in your vehicle. This will make spur-of-the-moment walking excursions fast and easy. Gather the following items and place them in a sturdy canvas bag or box for your car (place bottled items in a clear zippered plastic bag in case of spillage). Check the items periodically to make sure they have not run out, spilled out, or dried out before departing on your day trip.

- Sunscreen—body, scalp, face, lips
- Insect repellent—look for milder, child-friendly versions
- Hand sanitizer
- First aid kit—available at drug and discount stores
- Kleenex—good substitute for toilet paper if needed
- Extra pairs of clean white socks in case shoes and socks get muddy on your walk
- Extra pairs of slip-on shoes in case shoes get muddy
- Rain gear—umbrellas and rain jackets or ponchos
- Backpack to carry items on your walk
- Unopened bottled water
- Plastic bags to place muddy items in
- Cell phone, fully charged
- Camera with extra batteries and memory card
- Flashlight with extra batteries
- Binoculars
- Compass
- Writing journal
- This book!

On the day of your outing, check your walking package to make sure items have not run out, spilled out, or dried out. Check that your phone is charged up and extra batteries for your camera and flashlight are packed. Pack additional water bottles for each person walking. Pack a minimum of one liter of water for each person in your group. If it is going to be a warm day, pack a gallon of water in a cooler with ice or blue ice. Keep in mind that water bottles can also usually be refilled at park water fountains.

Always take snacks with you on your walk. Some high-energy suggestions: dried fruit, nuts, granola, protein bars, cheese cubes, whole wheat crackers, beef or turkey jerky or peanut butter with celery. Even if you are only going for a short walk, take snacks and water bottles. We found ourselves, more often than not, out on our walk far longer than we anticipated due to some offshoot path we wished to explore, lingering longer at a nature feature or discovering another area to explore. We were always glad to have a snack to sustain us so that we did not feel rushed to get back. If, after reading ahead about your planned walk, packing a lunch seems a good idea, consider taking sandwiches, cold chicken tenders, hard-cooked eggs, fresh fruit, cut-up veggies and hummus, whole-grain crackers with cheese, and whole-grain cookies or dried dates or other fruit. Pack these items in a cooler with ice for after your walk. Or, if taking a picnic with you on your walk, transfer items to your backpack with a soft blue-ice pack or two. For sandwiches, use toasted, thick-sliced whole-grain bread, coated with butter, olive oil, or coconut oil to keep the bread from getting soggy. Consider soft juice pouch drinks for a carry-along lunch. Last, if you are heading out in the late afternoon or evening, always take a flashlight (or, download a flashlight app on your smartphone ahead of time).

Don't forget your ice cream treat afterwards! Consider a light lunch and saving dessert for later. At the end of each section in this book, we have given suggestions for an ice cream treat nearby or on your way home. These stops just added to our enjoyment of our outing and especially of our time together. It is our fervent wish that you cherish your time in the great outdoors with people you care about as much as we have while walking these wonderful nature paths.

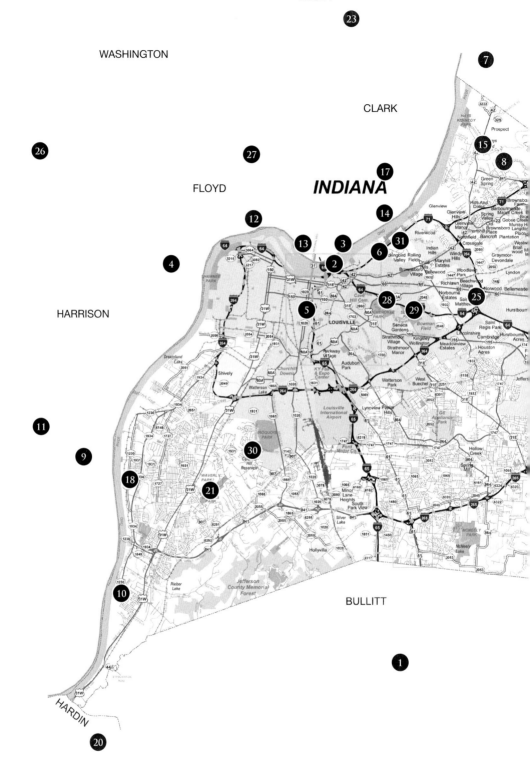

MAP OF EXCURSIONS

1   Bernheim Arboretum and Forest

BIG FOUR BRIDGE
2   Kentucky Side: Louisville Waterfront Park
3   Indiana Side: Jeffersonville Big Four Station Park

4   Campbell Woodland Nature Trails
5   Central Park and St. James Court
6   Champions Park
7   Creasey Mahan Nature Preserve
8   Harrods Creek Park
9   Hayswood Nature Reserve: Indian Creek Trail
10 Kulmer Beach Reserve
11 O'Bannon Woods State Park: Tulip Valley Trail

OHIO RIVER GREENWAY
12 New Albany at Riverfront Park
13 Clarksville at Falls of the Ohio

14 Perrin Family Park
15 Putney Pond and Woodlands
16 Red Orchard Park
17 Richard L. Vissing Park
18 Riverview Park

19 THE PARKLANDS OF FLOYDS FORK
    The Louisville Loop in Beckley Creek Park
    Coppiced Woods Trail
    Sycamore Trail and Egg Lawn Path
    Humana Grand Allee Country Lane Walk
    Valley of the Giants Trail

20 Saunders Springs Nature Preserve
21 Waverly Park
22 Wendell Moore Park
23 William Graham Park: Lake Iola Walking Patk

ADDITIONAL WALKING PATHS FROM
TAKE A HIKE, LOUISVILLE!
24 Anchorage Park
25 Brown Park and Arthur K. Draut Park
26 Buffalo Trace Park
27 Sam Peden Community Park
28 Cherokee Park—Baringer Hill Path
29 Seneca Park
30 Iroquois Park
31 Thurman Hutchins Park

Map courtesy of the Commonwealth of
Kentucky Transportation Cabinet.

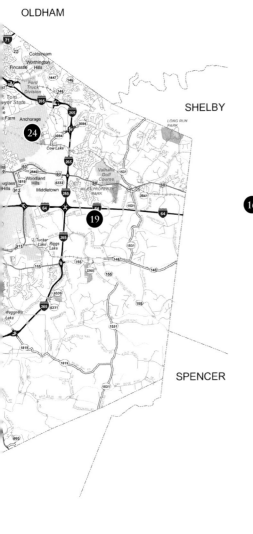

OLDHAM

SHELBY

SPENCER

BERNHEIM ARBORETUM AND FOREST

BULLITT COUNTY, KENTUCKY

Walking Path: One to three miles, paved, gravel, and dirt trails; mostly accessible.

Features: Scenic parklands, big prairie meadow, woodland trails, garden paths, lakes and streams.

Facilities: Restrooms inside Visitor Center and Education Center.

Getting there: I-65 South from Louisville. Bernheim Arboretum and Research Forest is located 20 minutes south of Louisville; take Exit 112 from I-65. Head east for approximately one mile on Highway 245 (KY S. R. 245/Clermont Road); the entrance is on the right-hand side of the road.

Note: There is a $5.00 per carload entrance fee for nonmembers. (It is well worth it!).

http://bernheim.org/

No walking guide to Louisville area nature paths and walking trails would be complete without a section dedicated to the beautiful grounds and natural areas available to explore in Bernheim Forest (officially known as Bernheim Arboretum and Research Forest). It is one of our all-time favorite places to explore and connect with nature. There is so much to love within the boundaries of this natural resource treasure. We have always felt blessed to have such a serene and peaceful place so near to Louisville to relax, picnic, walk, hike, and connect with the outdoors.

Bernheim is a walker's paradise. There are multiple options for walkers of all ages and abilities. For families with small children, there are short nature trails including the "I Spy" trail located behind the Education Center and the "Fairy Trail" alongside the Visitor Center, plus our favorite playground in the world, the Children's Play Garden, located in Guerilla Hollow. For middle-age kids, there are

"I walked slowly, and carefully held onto the railing to see the view over the trees."

more challenging hiking trails in the natural forest area, the Canopy Tree Walk, and Lookout Tower. For seniors, the Sun and Shade Trail and Lake Nevin Loop offer serene and scenic walks through gardens and woodlands and along the lake. There are many wonderful paths and trails, and it is hard to pick a favorite. It seems that every time we visit, there are new trails to explore. We simply love this place, and you will too.

On a recent springtime visit, we were blessed with a warm, sunny, and breezy early May afternoon. We were hoping to catch some beautiful spring blooms, and we were not disappointed. Dainty pink and white hybrid dogwoods and bright magenta azaleas offered a breathtaking treat for the eyes.

We began our visit, as always, at the Visitor Center. We parked in the side lot, then walked over the boardwalk under the canopy of giant evergreen trees up to the entrance of the center. We were delighted to read signs informing us of the upcoming opening of the Edible Garden, located across from the Visitor Center. We made a note to come back soon to explore this new attraction.

The Visitor Center is a great place to start your visit, because you can pick up a free trail map and get information from the helpful attendants. We always stop at the koi pond and small waterfall outside the center. Inside, there is a café at the center serving lunch and other refreshments. We made a note to return for ice cream after our excursion.

We planned to do several short walks this day, covering different areas of the forest and breaking up our day with a picnic lunch. From the Visitor Center, we walked out of the back of the center to enter the delightful Fairy Walk.

This is a short, paved connecting trail through shady woods. Bernheim holds fairy house-building events periodically. Children and adults are encouraged to build forest fairy houses made out of natural building materials such as twigs, branches, stones, rocks, leaves, pinecones, sweet gum pods, logs, and other forest finds. Previously built fairy houses line the path and are hidden under low branches tucked back off the trail a bit. They are delightful and whimsical. We never miss this walk to see what new creations have been placed there for the forest fairies. Signs encourage visitors not just to observe, but also repair any that are in disrepair. This walk always encourages our daughter to build her own fairy house in the woods around our own home when we return.

After descending through this short walk, you will emerge at the Two Ponds area and will see the trail and a sign indicating the Two Ponds Loop, which encircles the two small lakes and passes through the holly grove. This is approximately a 30-minute walk, seven miles in distance.

After completing this lovely loop, we crossed the bridge over the two ponds and then crossed the road (Arboretum Way) to ascend the hill up to the Education Center.

The Education Center is not to be missed, especially if there are children in your group. We always enjoy a visit to this center, which houses a lovely bird blind (we never pass up an opportunity to sit in a bird blind and observe our winged friends for a few minutes), lots of educational flyers, and hands-on nature activities geared to children. On this day, we were cajoled by our young daughter to reassemble a large, three dimensional topographical floor puzzle, which was a map of the forest area. This very challenging activity was taking a bit too long for our liking, so we had to resort to a small bit of cheating by looking under the pieces for numbers helping us place the pieces in the right positions (shh, don't tell anyone).

Picking up a pamphlet at the center, we were intrigued to learn more about the "I Spy" trail behind the Education Center. We took a list of items to find along the trail and went outside to begin. The idea is to use your observation skills to pick out items that don't belong in the natural dense woods. The trail goes in two directions behind the Education Center. We walked the short trail up and back several times and still did not find all the items on the list. But we did find many, including a Chinese take-out box, straw, pencil, wooden paint stirrer, sunglasses, deflated balloon, bottle, small flag, flashlight, plastic slinky, kid's bracelet, and even a cheese grater. This experience encourages walkers to really slow down and take a good look into the natural woods. The path is a hiking trail through the woodland, so be aware of roots and rocks in the path. It's well worth the effort; the woods are beautiful, and the path descends to a rustic bridge, allowing your group to experience a very scenic short hike.

From here, we walked back the way we came (approximately a half mile) to our car, which we had left parked at the Visitor Center.

After our morning of hiking and educational endeavors, we were ready for lunch. We had brought a picnic lunch and looked forward to relaxing at the Guerilla Hollow area, where a lovely picnic area and the wonderful Children's Play Garden awaited.

From the Visitor Center, follow Visitor Center Drive to the east and pick up Arboretum Way. Turn left onto Guerilla Hollow Road and follow the signs to the Guerilla Hollow Picnic Area. Find a parking spot along the road. The picnic area is adjacent to the Children's Play Garden. There are lots of picnic tables close to the road so you will probably not have to carry your picnic items too far. Grills are available for cookouts.

We carried in our picnic and enjoyed a shady lunch under the towering trees. After lunch, we found much to enjoy in the Play Garden (yes, we are kids at heart). Along with traditional wooden play structures and swings, the Garden includes nature-themed activities like tree-stump jumping and sturdy, twisted-twig houses for children and adults alike. There is also a shaded pavilion to enjoy, funded by the Eleanor Grigsby Fund for the Elderly. If you have children in your party, allow at least an hour for lunch and playtime in this unique area.

We had several more adventures planned for the afternoon, including a foray into the natural forest area, so we headed back to our car. Our destination was the Canopy Tree Walk.

To reach this area, drive out of Guerilla Hollow and turn right on Arboretum Way, then right again on Forest Hill Drive. This is the wild and scenic woodland area of Bernheim, and you will thoroughly enjoy this majestic drive. You will be traveling uphill for approximately a mile and a half. Take a left at the one way loop and look for the sign for the Canopy Tree Walk on your left. You will park on the right. The path leading to the overlook structure is across the road from the parking area.

Follow a short trail to the Canopy Tree Walk, which is an elevated boardwalk extending into the forest canopy, 75 feet above the forest floor. Walk out onto the structure for a spectacular view. If you have a fear of heights, be aware that the structure sways a bit and can be a bit disconcerting as it offers a view above the tree line not normally experienced, even on ascending trails. As I do have a fear of heights, I walked slowly, and carefully held onto the railing for views over the trees. Most will not have a problem and will enjoy this unusual experience.

We had one more walk planned for our day, so we returned to our vehicle and descended out of the natural woodlands to Arboretum Way. Our last walk would be along the Sun and Shade trail.

At Arboretum Way, turn left and look for parking areas on the left, across from Big Prairie. We parked near the spiral sculpture and picked up the Sun and Shade Loop trail at that point. This loop runs through a beautiful landscaped area and also through a natural woodland area adjacent to Lake Nevin. Walking along this three-quarter-mile path reminds one of the spectacular landscaping of the gardens at the Biltmore Estate in North Carolina. And for good reason: Biltmore's spectacular landscaping was designed by American's foremost landscape architect, Frederick Law Olmsted, whose landscape architecture firm also designed the gardens in Bernheim Forest.

In this area, you will find examples of trees and shrubs that can grow in a range of light conditions. We walked along the landscaped path, enjoying the scents of flowering shrubs and the buzz of bees out enjoying the springtime as much as we were. We approached Lake Nevin and observed the sparkling lake, lively with small ripples from the stiff breeze. We found a bench to sit and soak up the sun and enjoy the tranquility that is so much a part of the Bernheim experience.

After resting near the lake a bit, we backtracked along the gravel trail and picked up the paved part of the trail again. I enjoyed gazing across the roadway and soaking up the expansive views of Big Meadow and the forested hill beyond. Continuing along, the trail winds through the woodland area and becomes a hiking trail. If you have mobility issues, simply walk along the paved trail and avoid the gravel or dirt portions. There is something for everyone on the Sun and Shade Loop.

We found the spiral statue and reluctantly headed back to our car. Leaving beloved Bernheim at day's end is always the hardest part for us. However, our youngster was anxious for her ice cream treat, so we drove back up to the Visitor Center and made it just in time for ice cream at Isaac's Café, which closed at 4:00 p.m. that day. If you miss this deadline, your alternative is to leave the forest and stop at the Valero gas station on your way back to I-65. You will be relegated to an ice cream bar out of the freezer case, but on a hot day, it will suffice. And it will allow you to linger a little longer in the peace and beauty of Bernheim Forest.

BIG FOUR BRIDGE

KENTUCKY SIDE: LOUISVILLE WATERFRONT PARK
JEFFERSON COUNTY, KENTUCKY

Walking Path: Two miles round-trip,
paved, completely accessible.

Features: Walk along and over the Ohio River on the
repurposed Big Four Pedestrian Bridge.

Facilities: Restrooms at parking areas during hours of operation.

Getting there: 1101 River Road in Louisville.

Note: The Big Four Bridge may be closed with
winter weather or when there is snow and ice on the bridge.

http://www.louisvillewaterfront.com/projects/big_four/

For over 70 years, from 1895 to 1969, the Big Four Bridge carried trains from St. Louis, Cleveland, Chicago, and Cincinnati across the Ohio River between Louisville, Kentucky and Jeffersonville, Indiana. After the bridge went out of commission in 1969, its original approaches were removed, and it sat idle for 40 years, earning the nickname, "the bridge that goes nowhere."

In 2011, Kentucky Governor Steve Beshear and Indiana Governor Mitch Daniels announced that the two states, along with the City of Jeffersonville, would allocate funding to convert the Big Four Bridge to a pedestrian and bicycle path across the river. A pedestrian ramp on the Kentucky side was opened in February of 2013, and the Jeffersonville ramp opened in May of 2014.

We were very excited to make an excursion to see for ourselves what all of the buzz had been about for years, as the work on the entrance ramps to the "new" pedestrian bridge was underway. Any new walking option in our area always piques our interest, and we had a great feeling about this one.

"A beautiful blue sky with wispy swirling clouds and a distant sun shining through presented itself."

We headed out for our walk on an early fall evening. Our adult son, who lives on the Kentucky side in an apartment complex near Waterfront Park, suggested we time our visit for a sunset view along the river, and we took him up on that suggestion. We were certainly not disappointed. We suggest you do the same. On this evening, we checked the sunset time by googling "sunset time" and it popped right up for our local area. Sunset was shown as 7:50 p.m., so we planned to arrive an hour prior. On this nice evening, we should have been prepared for crowds, but were not.

Parking can be tricky, as this is a very popular spot. As you drive along River Road, look for the large circular ramp leading up to the bridge, and then try to find a spot in one of the parking areas—there are several on the river side and one on the opposite side. Be prepared to circle around these lots until you see someone pull out to get a space. Parking is also allowed along River Road.

Once we found our spot in a lot on the river side, we got out and headed toward the river. We turned west at the police boat station and followed the sidewalk, passing the amphitheater on the left. Next we walked by the old Tumbleweed Restaurant site (as of this writing, the restaurant was scheduled to close), and the unique waterfront playground and splash park. The water was still pumping out onto the splash grounds from fish mouths and spurting up from ground level—even though it was well into October. If you are walking with children, they will no doubt want to stop and play. Promise them a romp in the splash ground when you return from your walk on the bridge.

Several bench-type swings overlook the river, and the adults in our group wanted to stop for a rest but decided to wait until after our walk.

One thing we missed on our way up to the bridge—but found on our way back—is a ramp leading to a river overlook at the point where you see a large set of steps leading up to the bridge. Take this side visit out to the river. It provides a beautiful view of the bridge you will be walking on, and gets you up close and out on the water.

The set of steps up to the bridge's ramp is in front of you—you can take them up, or walk south through the parking area (toward River Road) to arrive at the beginning of the spiral ramp up to the bridge. This is the accessible entrance. You will now start a long, slow incline up to the top. Be aware: this can be a challenge, even for adults in good physical shape. Go slow and hold on to the rail. Take breaks when you need and enjoy the view at each turn. This is a quarter-mile ramp. The swing garden is visible below as you walk up—a unique part of the park you may wish to visit when you come back down.

As we walked up, a barge's horn sounded from the river. A beautiful blue sky with wispy swirling clouds and a distant sun shining through presented itself to us, on its way to the end of the day. The river flowed beneath, wide and timeless. The Louisville skyline grew prettier, too, the higher up the ramp we went.

It will get breezier as you approach the top of the bridge. You may wish to bring a jacket in the summer and a heavier coat as it gets later in the year. Bicycles, strollers, motorized wheelchairs, roller skates, and even Segways are allowed on the bridge. One thing that is not allowed is pets. The authorities took away pet access in the early days of the bridge's opening due to the amount of pet waste being neglected by careless owners.

At the top of the ramp, we found a concession stand selling hot dogs, snacks, and ice cream. Yes! Our ice cream treat was in reach. Conversing with the two very personable young men running the stand, we were informed that it is called "Dogs on the Run," and offers Orange Leaf frozen yogurt—one of our favorites—as well as Blue Bunny ice cream treats. Not wanting to risk the stand closing before we came back from our walk, and unable to resist Orange Leaf, we made a rare exception to our rule and purchased our frozen treat before finishing our walk. It turned out to be the right choice, as we very much enjoyed this walk and being able to enjoy the creamy caramel apple treat as we walked—it was the perfect combination of cold treat plus a yummy fall flavor. Turns out we needn't have worried, though, as Dogs on the Run is usually open until 10 p.m. on summer nights. They also operate out of an Airstream trailer near the Splash Park and have plans to have an outlet on the Jeffersonville side as well. The other good news is we were told that in cooler months, they will offer hot chocolate and apple cider. We were so happy to have these treats at our fingertips, we almost forgot the reason we were here. On to the walk.

The bridge stretched in front of us seemingly forever. Benches are available every few feet. Lights swing down from the overhead trusses. We seemed to be walking very high above the water. Don't look down if you get dizzy or are a little afraid of heights. I am, but it did not detract from my enjoyment of this awesome walk. As you approach the middle of the bridge, you will hear music coming from speakers above. On the night we walked, it was American marching band music. It felt a little incongruous to me. Personally, I could have done without this, as I enjoy the sounds of nature better—the wind and water would have been enough for me. I had to admit, however, that the music lent itself to a sense of accomplishment for making it thus far.

We continued walking toward the Jeffersonville side. We could hear music coming from the Jeffersonville RiverStage amphitheater below, where a concert was playing. It was a very festive atmosphere below and above.

The sun was nearly down when we came to the Indiana side of the bridge. On this night, a metal gate blocked us from going farther, but we are happy to report that since then, the Jeffersonville side is fully open and one can walk on down into the town on the Indiana side if one wishes.

Below, on the Jeffersonville side, we could see it was very different from the Louisville side. Pretty, old-fashioned homes lined the street below. It was much quieter than the Louisville side, and we could see some folks fishing off a circular stone wall below. We were surprised there was no one fishing off the bridge itself; with the breeze, you could really throw a line out far into the river.

It was getting darker, and we wondered when the lights would come on as we turned around and headed back to the Louisville side. A very loud speedboat whizzed by below; we figured he was doing at least 60. Probably illegal, said the young adult walking with us. Never a dull moment on this walk.

The bridge once again seemed to stretch forever as we headed back, but a slow and steady gait, and the lights finally coming on, led to a very pleasant walk back. It came all too soon, actually; we were sorry to reach the end. The colorful lights of the city reflected in the river below and the beautiful orange-peach dusky sunset illuminated our way down the circular ramp. We had timed it just right. A lovely half-moon showed through the wispy clouds as our evening came gradually to a close. It was the perfect end to our weekend; we could not wait to come back.

Big Four Bridge

Walking Path: Two miles round-trip, paved, completely accessible.

Features: Walk through a city park and over the Ohio River on the repurposed Big Four Bridge.

Facilities: Restroom building at Big Four Station Park

Getting there: From Louisville, I-65 N to Exit 0. Right on Court Avenue, right on Spring. Parking on Spring Street, public parking lot at corner of Spring and Chestnut, or at Big Four Station parking lot on West Market Street.

Note: The Big Four Bridge may be closed during winter weather or when there is snow and ice on the bridge.

http://www.jeffparks.org

We were thrilled when the Jeffersonville side of the Big Four Bridge finally opened to pedestrians in May of 2014. Now that the bridge is open on both sides of the river, a wonderful walking experience is provided from either side. Many Louisville folks are now walking over to Jeffersonville and discovering shops, historic buildings, eateries and taverns well worth exploring. Jeffersonville residents can head over to Louisville on foot, or cycle.

Since we live in Indiana, we were happy not to have to drive across the river to walk on the bridge. We picked a warm and sunny summer afternoon to walk over the bridge from the Jeffersonville side for the first time.

We parked on Spring Street with the thought that we would stop for our ice cream treat at Schimpff's Confectionary after our walk. Schimpff's has an old-

"The ramp is a long gracefully curving S-shaped incline of one-quarter mile."

fashioned ice cream soda fountain. We were disappointed to learn that the shop is closed on Sunday, the day we were walking. We continued on toward the bridge, hoping to find an alternative.

We walked up Chestnut Street toward the ramp, taking a side trip to visit a delightful small public garden enclosed in a brick courtyard. This is a surprising hidden gem. Stone paths wind through a shade garden surrounded by brick walls. Benches offer a spot to rest, away from the hot sun. Our youngster enjoyed trying out every bench in the garden and delighted in chasing after a bright, yellow-striped salamander that had scrambled up one of the garden walls.

After this interesting side trip to the small hidden garden, we continued up Chestnut Street, gawking up at the beautiful, 100-year-old National Historic Register buildings along the way. Another surprising bonus—and we hadn't even reached the bridge yet!

And then, yet another bonus as we spotted a cute frozen yogurt shop (Treats) on Pearl Street almost at the base of the ramp. We simply could not resist purchasing tubs of frozen yogurt to take up on the bridge with us, once again breaking our tradition of walking first, ice cream last. We didn't want to risk the shop being closed when we returned (we needn't have worried—Treats stays open until 9 p.m.; closed on Mondays).

So, with Hawaiian pineapple and vanilla yogurt with sprinkles in tow, we finally made it up to the Big Four Station park-in-progress, which is where the ramp to the Big Four Bridge is located. On this day, the park was still being developed, with just the skeleton structures in place. Since then, we are happy to report that the park is now fully open, with water features, playground, picnic pavilion, green space, and a restroom building. The ramp is open up to the bridge and an alternative, a set of stairs, is also available. A planned elevator has not materialized at this writing.

The ramp is a long (quarter-mile), gracefully curving S-shaped incline. There are no pets allowed (but dates, romance, and fun are allowed, according to the Jeffersonville Parks Department signage). We walked it slowly, enjoying the views over the railing on the way up.

We made it up to the bridge, frozen yogurt long gone on this hot July afternoon. But at the top, a delightfully brisk breeze across the river cooled us off. We were familiar with the walk across the bridge, as we had walked it several times from the Louisville side. On this day, the middle lane was filled with bikes: three-wheeled pedal vehicles holding three passengers each, and tandem bikes too. Their helpful warning bells alerted us slower walkers to move out of the bike lane.

We approached the midsection of the bridge where the piped-in music can be heard. Today, it was classical music (our last walk featured marching band music). We took a moment to gaze out toward the northeast at the impressive, mighty Ohio. We were enjoying the explosion of nature up along this unique walk with wind, sun, and the sparkling river below.

We walked to the Louisville side, so excited to realize that now people can actually walk from one side of the river all the way over to the other side—we can cross over to another state on foot if we choose. Of course, there was no car waiting for us on that side, so we turned and walked back to "our" side of the river. The bridge is a half mile long, so a walk over and back is one mile. Adding the two ramps adds another mile (a quarter mile each).

On the ramp back down to the Jeffersonville side, our wonderful breeze let up, and we faced a long, hot and sunny walk back to our car. Note that there is no shade yet, as the park is not finished. Bring water! The steps and elevator were not open yet either, so there was no alternative but to keep walking and sweating back to our car. Traipsing back down the longer ramp was a small price to pay for such a wonderful walking experience; we knew we'd return soon.

CAMPBELL WOODLAND NATURE TRAILS

FLOYD COUNTY, INDIANA

Walking Path: Approximately one mile, paved, completely accessible.

Features: Woodlands, bridges over creeks, small waterfall. Accessible trail and picnic table. Solar-powered audio kiosk explaining the park's history.

Facilities: Portable restroom at trailhead.

Getting there: I-64 West from Louisville toward New Albany, take the first exit over the Sherman Minton. Merge onto Elm, take a right at Scribner Drive. Three cross streets to a right on Main Street, which continues onto River Road/ IN 111. After .6 mile, turn right onto Budd Road. Drive 2.2 miles to 3300 Budd Road. When you see the Harvest Time Tabernacle church on the right, you are just about there. The park is on the right. There is a small parking area.

http://www.floydcountyparks.org

After winding along Budd Road for what felt like way more than two miles, we found this relatively new, 122-acre Floyd County nature park. We pulled into a small but well-maintained parking area marked with colorful, easy-to-read signage. We were here on a muggy late summer evening, hoping for a cool respite in the green woodlands. We were not disappointed.

We noticed that there are no restroom facilities at the parking area, but there is an entrance to the trails. We also noted that we had no cell service. At the trailhead, three-tenths of a mile from the parking area, we found portable facilities, as well as an accessible table under a small pavilion.

We sprayed ourselves with bug spray as we were walking into the evening; mosquitos would likely be out before we finished our walk. We grabbed our water bottles too, knowing we'd need them on this humid evening.

"The magic healing power of nature was upon me once again."

Signage at the parking area provided a bit of information on the park. The property was once owned by Paul S. Campbell, who, at his death ten years ago, declared his last wish that his land be designated for public use.

The paved access trail starts out from the parking area. It is a multiuse, paved and lined roadway for walking and biking and for access vehicles (speed limit is posted at 15 mph). The path starts out at a gentle uphill ascent. The woodlands are dense on both sides of the path, offering an immediate dose of deep greenery. However, the remains of a dumping ground is visible in a gully on the east side. Old tires, chicken wire, trash, scrap wood, and the like, are slowly being taken over by the natural vegetation. The dumping ground is private property abutting this access path to the woodlands.

A nice resin bench is available if this first climb requires a break. Here the woods get a bit quieter and the road noise starts to become muffled. I felt the stress of the day begin to dissipate as my breathing deepened and the sounds of the birds and a gentle breeze ruffling the branches reached my senses. A small streambed is below the path. Not much water was flowing in the stream on this hot summer night—just a still pool of water, good for the frogs, which were starting to chirp.

Continuing on our uphill march to the trailhead, we found another well-placed bench. This stopping point held a nicer view of the rocky streambed below. Here we stopped to read the *Trail Rules* sign. We were instructed not to feed the wildlife, keep all pets on a leash, bring in no firearms, not to hunt, and that no motorized vehicles save wheelchairs are allowed.

A bit more to climb, and we were nearing the trailhead. Tall sprigs of wild purple phlox lined the path, and a bumblebee buzzed from stalk to stalk looking for a quick sip of nectar. We didn't blame him—it was hot and we sipped from our water bottles frequently.

Here the environment turned to deeper woods; the sounds of civilization now far removed. My breathing slowed as the stresses from my work day began to dissipate. I always enjoy inhaling deep breaths of forest air and exhaling slowly, releasing whatever tension I may be harboring. Works every time, and tonight was no exception. The magic healing power of nature was upon me once again.

The sun was beginning to set behind the western ridge along the path, and our photographer hurried ahead to snap a few pics of the lovely path and woodlands before losing the light of the day.

The blacktop leads over a bridge, crossing a rocky stream. There was no trickle of water in sight or sound tonight. A bank rises steeply on the west side, where yellow wildflowers lit up the dense forest greenery. We were still going uphill, and my thighs gave a small protest, but just a little.

The mosquitos were definitely buzzing around us, and we were glad we had sprayed before starting out. Over a second bridge, we looked below to see a small bit of water movement and realized how pretty these streamed views would be after a good spring rain. I made a mental note: come back in the cool spring after a good soaking rain. The environment here will be like a rain forest.

We had already enjoyed a good bit of nature and exercise as we ended just this first stretch to reach the trailhead and now we were at a split in the path. Here was the solar-powered kiosk—operated by pushing four different buttons to listen to parts of the history of the park. We heard about the financing and grants that were put together to create this outdoor recreation facility for the people of Floyd County and about plans to add more trails in the future. A nice touch.

This open area normally offers a great view of the creek, but on this evening, we were disappointed that weedy overgrowth blocked the great view. If we had not known about it from a previous visit, we would have pushed on through to the trail and missed it completely. There is a large rock in the middle of the grassy area that our youngster claimed was perfect for sitting and reading. . Here there is also a park map, accessible picnic table, and restroom facilities. There is no running water, however.

A red gate marks the start of the actual Campbell Woodland nature trails area. The blacktop road gives way here to an inviting, smooth concrete walking path that snakes through the woods. This portion is a three-quarter-mile loop taking you through more open woodlands and areas of taller trees. We noted and appreciated that the parks department had recently mown both sides of the path, opening up a wide, weed-free walk.

Along the trail are two rustic wooden walking bridges crossing the pebbly stream. I don't know what it is about rustic bridges along woodland paths, but I love them, as do most nature hikers. The more rustic the better—leaving to the imagination the possibility that they were built by fairies, gnomes, elves, or some other creatures of the forest.

We were deep in the forest land now, and our 11-year-old said, "It's so peaceful out here . . . except for that squeaking noise." What noise? As soon as I thought it, I realized she was being a bit sarcastic about my walking sandals squishing and squeaking with each step, interrupting our nature sounds interlude. Another note to self: Next walk, wear quieter shoes.

The path continues to wind through shady woods. At the second bridge, be sure to look over the railing to the pond below. On a previous visit, several large bullfrogs had been visible, alas, none tonight. Around a bend, the cutout through an upland meadow is visible, indicating the eventual extension of this trail. We kept on the established loop on this visit, considering exploring that unfinished trail on another visit.

Tulip poplars and sweet gum trees were some standouts we noted as we wound our way back on the loop path. Our daughter loves picking up the sweet gum pods—and a few had already fallen on this late summer evening. They are her "fairy chandeliers," as she calls them.

I looked up in appreciation at some of the soaring trees in the park. I really love large old trees. The sun had set now behind the ridge, and our photographer had reluctantly put away his camera. We savored the last bits of light, along with the calm, quiet nature walk. My last note to self: we need to do this more often on weeknights. Why wait for the weekend?

Gracie asked if we would still have time for our ice cream treat, worried that walking on a school night would not allow it. "Oh yes," I tell her, "We did the trail, didn't we?" And I know the perfect place.

Polly's Freeze, a local favorite roadside ice cream stand, is located at 5242 Indiana 62, a short drive up Corydon Pike from IN 111. As it was nearly on the way home for us, it was a natural for our ice cream treat. To get there, drive back along Budd Road to IN 111 the way you arrived, then veer left at the stop light. Head up Corydon Pike, three miles to the end. Turn left on IN 62 and Polly's Freeze is a half mile on the right. You can't miss the bright neon Polly's sign. This place is an icon for local residents and widely considered one of the best roadside soft-serve ice cream eateries in the country. You really don't want to miss it. We enjoyed flurries and sugar-free, coffee-flavored frozen yogurt sitting at a concrete table under the stars. A summer evening couldn't get much better.

When you are finished, go back on IN 62, past Corydon Pike to I-64 straight ahead for a faster drive back to New Albany or Louisville.

CENTRAL PARK AND ST. JAMES COURT

JEFFERSON COUNTY, KENTUCKY

Walking Path: 1.5 miles, paved stone, brick, and concrete. Completely accessible.

Features: Parkland, old-growth landscaped trees, Victorian mansions and gardens.

Facilities: Restroom building at park. Open seasonally.

Getting there: Fourth Street and Park Avenue in downtown Louisville. Head south from downtown on Third or Fourth Street. Travel seven to eight blocks and turn onto Park, Magnolia or Hill Street. Park along any of these streets (for this walk, we parked on Sixth Street near Hill). St. James Court is just south of the park and adjacent to it.

http://www.louisvilleky.gov/MetroParks/parks/central/

Another "must-do" walk for this guide is a stroll through Louisville's oldest and most ornate park and neighborhood: Central Park and St. James Court, located in Old Louisville, just south of downtown.

Central Park is a 17-acre green jewel in the heart of Old Louisville. Today it is a municipal park maintained by the city of Louisville, but it has an interesting history: once a part of the du Pont family's estate, it was developed for public use in the 1870s and was the site of the famous Southern Expedition in the 1880s. During the five years of the exposition, 13 acres were roofed and used to showcase Thomas Edison's light bulb, one of the first public displays of the new technology. Later the park was unroofed and included an electric trolley, roller coaster, bicycle trails, an art museum, and a lake.

In 1904, the city enlisted famed architect Frederick Law Olmsted to plot a new public park. Olmsted had a large open-air shelter with a colonnade built on top

"Walking through it feels like walking through an ancient Roman ruin."

of the hill where the art museum once stood (the beautiful colonnade is still there today). He also included a wading pool, athletic fields, and walking trails.

In the 1970s, the shelter was converted to a police station and the Old Louisville information center, which are both still housed there today. In 1976, an amphitheater and wooden playhouse were built, today used for the free Shakespeare in the Park productions and other performances.

We headed out to explore the park and surrounding neighborhood on a warm and muggy midsummer evening. We were looking forward to a leisurely stroll and ice cream at the downtown Comfy Cow near the University of Louisville.

Having a college-age daughter living near St. James Court, we decided to park close to her apartment near Sixth and Hill Streets, and went first to visit with her and a new puppy. We decided to take the puppy with us on our walk. Our daughter was delighted with her new family addition, and we naturally all fell immediately in love with the minuscule Boston terrier puppy. She was happy to pack up puppy supplies, including a bottle of water and dish, puppy harness, blanket, and small plastic bags in case he did his business. She was also happy to show us a back way into St. James Court, Belgravia Court, and Central Park—all beautiful and accessible areas to walk or jog.

We started out around the corner from her apartment on Hill Street and walked a few steps north up Sixth Street. We turned right onto Belgravia Court, which runs perpendicular to the southernmost end of St. James Court.

Turning into this court, prepare to be stunned at its beauty. It has been described as the most beautiful of Old Louisville's walking courts, and I would have to agree. Belgravia opens on each end to Fourth and Sixth Streets (one may enter from either end). The court is almost hidden from view—you can't see it from a drive-by. It is tucked away from the noises of the city, offering a quiet, peaceful walk among gorgeously preserved Victorian homes facing each other across a green area decked out with flowering plants and statuary.

After enjoying the walk around Belgravia, we were anxious to see St. James Court, home to the area's largest annual art show, The St. James Court Art Show, which takes place every October. The art show is many local residents' only experience of this beautiful neighborhood, and while a wonderful event, the boisterous crowds of the art show often preclude the walker (and gawker) from enjoying long, leisurely looks at the beautiful Victorian architecture and gardens.

As we emerged onto St. James, I have to admit I was a bit awed as I gazed at the ornate mansions and the beautiful center green space in the court in front of me. I felt truly mesmerized and taken back to another time. Our 20-year-old, who enjoys a nightly run in the area, said she feels as if she is in another city, another place and another time as she jogs through these wonderful old Victorian neighborhoods.

We started out on the south side of St. James Court heading north toward Central Park. Our walking plan for the evening was to go north on St. James, cross Magnolia into Central Park, and then circle back to walk up the other side of St. James back to Sixth and Hill, where we had parked.

The sidewalk along St. James is wide and covered with octagonal stones. As we walked, the St. James Court fountain, in the middle of the green, came into view. The calming and soothing sounds of splashing water serenaded our walk as we stared (some of us drooled) at the most ornate and stately of Old Louisville homes. We appreciated the shade offered by the old-growth leaf canopies high overhead. There is a sense of complete timelessness in this neighborhood; the lit gaslights lent an old-world ambiance to the evening as the sun began to set.

The walk along the court is level and lends itself to a leisurely pace. Strollers and wheelchairs will be just fine on this walk. Our slow pace on this evening was perfect for our small puppy companion, who walked along sniffing and stopping every foot or so.

We could not pick out a favorite among the Victorian mansions, each unique and beautiful, but the massive Bedford stone mansion, the Conrad-Caldwell House, on the corner of Magnolia and St. James at the entrance to Central Park, would be close to the top of anyone's list. This spectacular example of Richardsonian Romanesque architecture was the masterpiece of famed local architect Arthur Loomis of Clarke & Loomis. It was built in the early 1900s and features gargoyles, beautiful archways, elaborate stone designs, and magnificent stained-glass windows, making it completely stunning. Plan to stand and stare for a few minutes. From here, simply cross Magnolia Street to the south entrance of the beautiful Central Park.

As we entered the park this evening, we could hear musical strains coming from the direction of the playhouse and amphitheater. We assumed it was a Shakespeare in the Park production, but as we neared the area later in our walk, we found out that it was actually a chorus group performing a selection of Gilbert and Sullivan songs. They were part of the Gilbert and Sullivan Society of Louisville. At any rate, the accompaniment of old show tunes was a wonderful addition to our already pleasant evening stroll.

We chose to veer right at the entrance, anxious to walk among the deeply shaded green space and under the canopy of stately old-growth trees. According to our 20-year-old guide, an evening walk through the park is normally very quiet; we would have enjoyed that experience too, but on this night, the lovely human voices lifted in song were just as welcome.

There are park benches placed along the walking path—as always, we noted and appreciated those options to sit, rest, observe and just breathe in the scents of the outdoors, but we usually pass on that option, as we are out to get a little exercise and movement, and most often elect to continue walking.

We noted the unusual trees in this park—they are so old and well-maintained that they are almost fantastical. For me, the trees in Central Park are one of the most pleasing elements of this walk. They are huge, with long and thick snaking branches overhead. The leaf canopy is amazing, offering dark shade on even the brightest day. Take your time and walk slowly and allow your eyes to gaze upward.

Along this walkway in the park, you are once again surrounded by stately Old Louisville mansions. I continued to gawk at the beautiful homes, just as along St. James Court. We continued circling along the park's oval walkway and approached the tennis courts and playhouse. The evening sun slanted through the trees, casting a golden glow on the courts and on part of the amphitheater to our left.

The walkway continues up a small rise to the highest point in the park where the Du Pont mansion once stood. Today, the beautiful vine-covered portico with its stately columns runs along this high area. Walking through it feels like walking through an ancient Roman ruin. To the east is the amphitheater. We noted the picnic tables there, and one couple having a romantic candle-lit supper nearby. We could not think of a more romantic place and time to enjoy a picnic—on a lovely golden sunlit evening, under the canopy of hundred-year-old trees, next to an ancient ruin, with a chorus of pleasing voices serenading your time together.

At the end of the portico is the Old Louisville Visitor's Information Center and the police precinct building. On this evening, a few food and dessert trucks were lined up nearby, and we noted that there is also a concession offering alcoholic beverages (Will's Tavern) to enjoy during summer outdoor performances.

On the west side of the portico is a large playground and spray fountain. The fountain was in full force on this warm, muggy evening. Its spouting water splashing on the concrete spray ground, along with the laughter of several children enjoying its cooling drops, was our delightful serenade as we descended on the opposite side of the portico to continue our walk.

We strolled down the gently curving sidewalk behind the tennis courts enjoying some light cooling summer breezes. I continued to gawk at the amazing trees and beautiful gently rolling landscape, and turned back to the southeast to gaze at the imposing rooftop gables of the Conrad Caldwell House rising in the distance.

We walked down a set of steps to Sixth Street and turned south toward Magnolia Street; the direction from which we had come. The sidewalk here is the old rustic brick—very pretty, but a bit uneven, so watch your step. Pine boughs reached out over the sidewalk above us to touch the smaller trees on the opposite side, forming a lovely evergreen canopy that is enjoyable to walk through. Don't miss the huge walnut tree on the park side. It is a beautiful old-growth specimen, lovingly maintained, with gently curving branches and a huge, thick trunk. I am such a tree hugger, I couldn't help but stopping to stare at this beauty for a few minutes. We noted that this walk would naturally be spectacular decked out in fall splendor and vowed to return a few weeks later to witness it.

At Magnolia, we turned back up St. James Court and returned on the opposite side of the court. Again, we enjoyed the amazing ambiance of the beautiful, ornate mansions, lulled by the tinkling splashes of the water from the St. James Fountain. We noted the large and unique wood carving of "The Lamplighter," by local wood carver Rob Peterson, located on the east side of the fountain. After doing a bit of research later, we learned that the carving was created out of a 15-foot, 100-year-old oak stump that had been struck by lightning in the area. The sculpture was finished and dedicated in 2013.

At the fountain, we took a side trip to the east on Fountain Court, another of Louisville's famous old walking courts. This is another hidden garden cul-de-sac, with mansions facing each other across a green expanse with ornate planters filled with flowering plants, shaded hosta gardens and those ubiquitous old tall shade trees. Lovely indeed.

We circled back to St. James Court and finished up our walk through Belgravia Court, then headed back to Sixth and Hill Streets, where we had parked our vehicle.

This walk is like taking a wonderful trip back in time to Victorian Louisville through mansion courts and gardens. And it's all free for the walking! We are truly blessed to have this wonderful old preserved neighborhood and old-world central park in our city.

It was a very warm and muggy evening for our walk and we were ready for some ice cream. We had planned to head up toward Cardinal Town on the University of Louisville campus to the Comfy Cow, one of Louisville's very best ice creameries.

Comfy Cow is located at 339 Cardinal Boulevard, four blocks south of Hill Street. Our group enjoyed giant scoops of local-flavor ice cream including Monster Cookie Dough, Mint Julep, Chocolate Bourbon, Cake Batter Up, and the delightfully refreshing Watermelon Mint. Yum!

We congratulated ourselves on finding another fabulously enjoyable walk right beneath our noses!

CHAMPIONS PARK

JEFFERSON COUNTY, KENTUCKY

Walking Path: One to two miles, paved and gravel.

Features: Open meadow views, old-growth trees (remnants of old manicured golf course landscaping), meandering paths.

Facilities: Portable only; at entrance.

Getting there: Off I-71 at Zorn Avenue and River Road.

http://louisvilleky.gov/government/parks/park-list/ louisville-champions-park

This walking and dog run park was once the former River Road Country Club which housed a nine-hole golf course, tennis courts, large swimming pool and clubhouse. I remember coming to the country club back in the days when I was a *Courier-Journal* newspaper employee and my department held its annual Golf and Swim outing there. It was always a fun day away from the office (I would choose the leisurely poolside option instead of golfing), followed by a nice buffet dinner provided by the clubhouse. When the country club closed in 2005, I remember feeling a bit sad, but very glad that the Jefferson County Parks Department purchased the property to preserve it for recreational use as part of Champions Park, a 222-acre sports and recreational parklands area along River Road near Zorn Avenue.

"Remnants of the old golf course remain—a rustic bridge or shelter here, stone steps to nowhere there."

Plans for the property included sports fields, basketball courts, picnic shelters, and a spray/splash ground, none of which has yet materialized in 2014. A dog run opened near the location of the clubhouse in 2010 (register at Feeder's Supply for access to the dog run). Other than that, the park is simply an open area with meandering paths through the old golf course. We like it, though, because it offers a wonderful place to take a leisurely stroll, with or without your dog.

The walking trails are the old golf cart paths; they are for the most part still paved, but watch out for some rough patches. On the sunny spring afternoon of our visit, there were several families with dogs along the paths outside of the run. Several people allowed their dogs off leash, which is technically not allowed outside the run. As dog people ourselves, we didn't mind too much. If you are not a dog person, however, be aware that you may run into this concern.

Several paths wind through the park. Pick one and meander. We enjoyed the beautiful large old-growth trees, some in flower, remnants from a more manicured time. Our path crossed a small wooden bridge and wound around to an old rustic concession stand. The path ended, but we just crossed over a small area of grass and picked up another path heading in the same direction.

The back half of the park is a little quieter, even with the traffic noise of River Road nearby. Our young walker enjoyed coming upon old sand traps with enough leftover sand to stop and dig for a while. She decided to search for buried golf balls, and yes, she found a few. Her comment: "This is like a golf ball graveyard."

The paths tend to end suddenly, forcing one to look around for an alternate path which requires crossing the grass or old sand traps. Note to Parks Department: Please connect the walking paths.

At the back end of the park (near the soccer fields), there is a rise; we surmised that it was the old ninth hole. We climbed to the top and were rewarded with a nice, expansive view of the course we had just traversed. After pausing to enjoy the warming rays of spring sunshine, we headed down, returning along the wooded creek on the side opposite River Road.

We enjoyed this park for a number of reasons, the meandering paved paths, the variety of beautiful large old trees left over from the country club days, and the sense of abandonment and ruins left over from the recreational golf course. It gave us a feeling of *Spirited Away*, the Japanese anime film that begins in the ruins of an amusement park. We enjoyed exploring something with a vibrant history, now abandoned. Remnants of the old golf course remain for now—a rustic bridge or shelter here, stone steps to nowhere there. Be sure to get out and walk through these grounds now, before Mother Nature reclaims what is hers, as she is sure to do.

Note: We found out that local cross-country teams hold meets here regularly. You may want to check online before your visit to make sure there is nothing scheduled the day you wish to visit.

This park is none too challenging and is very enjoyable for a leisurely afternoon or evening stroll. For an ice cream treat after, you may want to head down to Waterfront Park and look for one of the ice cream truck vendors (seasonal summertime). The day of our visit in early spring, we headed up Zorn Avenue to Brownsboro Road and turned right to purchase ice cream sundaes at McDonald's drive-through. Perfect treats to savor for the drive home.

CREASEY MAHAN NATURE PRESERVE

OLDHAM COUNTY, KENTUCKY

Walking Path: Approximately two miles, gravel and grassy.

Features: Woodland garden with water features and rustic bridges; nature preserve paths through meadows and woodlands.

Facilities: Restroom building on the outside of the barn near entrance to Woodland Garden. Restrooms also available in the nature center.

Getting there: US 42 North to Goshen, Kentucky. Left on Highway 1793. Right on Harmony Landing. Park is on the left.

www.creaseymahannaturepreserve.org

Creasey Mahan Nature Preserve is one of our favorite nature destinations. We discovered it while researching our first book, *Take A Hike, Louisville!* It is a local favorite in the Goshen area and includes 170 acres of rolling woodlands, creeks, waterfalls, open meadows, and 9.5 miles of trails. The preserve is run by one of our favorite nature supporters and authors, Executive Director Tavia Cathcart Brown. She has done a spectacular job, adding amenities (such as the woodland garden) and family-friendly programming (such as the annual Nature of Christmas event) at the preserve to appeal to a wide spectrum of ages and abilities. On many previous visits, we fell in love with the unique features in the nature preserve, as well as the family-friendly nature center, seasonal events, and the historic homestead on the property. Be sure to check out the website before you visit and look for an event to attend as well as enjoying your nature walk while you are at the preserve.

Photo by Tavia Cathcart Brown

"The centerpiece of the garden includes a rock-strewn stream and waterfall. We enjoyed the sounds of the falling water almost as much as the view."

Our goal for our outing this day was to explore one of the preserve's newer features: the Woodland Garden, located just past the arbor into the forested trail area. . Created with the help of a grant the preserve received from the Barr Foundation, the Woodland Garden is designed to be a signature garden centerpiece encompassing six acres. . When completed, it will be one of the largest native wildflower and fern gardens in the United States.

We had a gorgeous crisp fall Saturday for a nature walk, with a deep blue sky and autumn color still holding strong in the trees. As we arrived and got out of our vehicle, we noted families pulling in, and kids and pets spilling out of SUVs. As we've mentioned, this is a well-loved nature preserve in the Goshen area.

Accessibility to the nature area is through an arbor to the north of the nature center. There is not a paved walkway, but a short walk up the gravel drive from the parking area and around the barn in the grassy area will put you at the entrance. Strollers and folks with walkers should not have too much trouble; if your group includes someone in a wheelchair, a little help may be needed.

The Woodland Garden is to the left of the arbor entrance. The paths through the garden are wide, well-marked and constructed of gravel and dirt. The paths meander through wildflower and fern beds. Stroll slowly and note the many varieties of plantings—all are identified with ground markers. On our visit, most flowers were finished blooming for the season, but we knew we would return in the spring to see them in their full glory. We noted the many native woodland plantings including foam flower, dwarf crested iris, lobelia, early meadow rue, trillium, bleeding hearts, green dragons, larkspur, and columbine, as well as lots of fern varieties.

Benches are placed conveniently around the garden. The staff at the preserve encourages folks to bring a snack and sit a spell on the benches to take in the lovely scenery.

The centerpiece of the garden is the water feature, which includes a rock-strewn stream and waterfall, with wooden bridges crossing over in several spots. It is very pretty to look at, and we enjoyed the sounds of the falling water almost as much as the view.

Walk slowly and watch for rocks and slippery leaves in the paths. Enjoy this lovely garden that blends into, and enhances, the beauty of the natural surroundings.

After getting your fill of the Woodland Garden, if you feel like stretching your legs a bit more, a good choice is to continue into the nature preserve trail area with a walk along the Mahan Lane path.

This stretch of path is relatively straight and flat. It is a dirt and grass trail. On a dry day, the surface will support your walker, stroller or wheelchair. As you continue down the lane, the Frog Pond comes into view almost immediately. Take a moment to read the interesting observation guide at the pond to learn about the many varieties of dragonflies.

The path continues through an open meadow on the west and woodlands on the east. Walking along this path on an early November morning, I enjoyed the crisp, clean air and the golds and reds of the trees. I loved hearing several woodland creatures scampering in the dry brush, and the sound of my own footfalls crunching the fallen leaves beneath my feet.

A family came up from the rolling wooded area pushing a stroller and singing "Old MacDonald" at the top of their lungs. I smiled a huge smile at their exuberance at being out in nature on such a glorious fall day. There is nothing in the world more perfect for a family to do on a beautiful fall day than to take a nature hike.

At the trail sign, you will need to make a choice of direction. Continuing straight will be a long downhill walk which may prove difficult for older walkers. If you need to stay on a flat path, simply turn back on Mahan Lane and enjoy your walk back to the entrance of the nature preserve.

We decided to turn left and meander along the Cross-Country Trail for a bit. We found a sign for the Sycamore Crest Trail which was to the left off of the Cross-Country Trail. This piece of the path leads to an old-growth sycamore tree, which is now unfortunately rotting away. Years ago, this had been a favorite tree for our daughter to climb in. There is a bench at the tree, which is a well-loved landmark. I rested here, enjoying the quiet and contemplating the circle of life.

The path circles back to Mahan Lane. Note that the trails can be a bit confusing to follow, but if you are on the Cross-County Trail side, do not worry; just meander and enjoy the gentle ups and downs and curves of the grassy meadow paths and you will eventually end up back on Mahan Lane.

We had brought a picnic this day and enjoyed it on the picnic tables located outside of the natural woodlands. Our daughter enjoyed swinging on the swings after lunch. Pets are more than welcome at the preserve; there is a dog fountain just for them. Please keep them on their leashes, though. After lunch, it was time to head out; our daughter made sure to remind us that we needed to save time for our ice cream treat. She never lets us forget her favorite part of these outings.

We headed back the way we came—toward Prospect on US 42, looking for ice cream. We noted a Dippin' Dots which is part of a Fuzzwig's Candy Factory shop on the left side, next to the Burning Bush Mediterranean Grill. That didn't really do it for us, so we kept going toward Prospect, where we found several great choices: Homemade Ice Cream and Pie Kitchen, located at 9561 US 42, Sweet Frog Premium Frozen Yogurt at 5909 Timber Ridge Drive (just off US 42) and our old standby, Dairy Queen (DQ) at 9515 US 42. I really wanted the Pie Kitchen, but the two younger members of our group won out with a double vote for Sweet Frog, where they enjoyed large bowls of frozen yogurt with several scoops of sweet toppings. We sat outside in the late afternoon sun to eat our frozen treats on the colorful Adirondack chairs, basking in the joy of our perfect outing.

HARRODS CREEK PARK

JEFFERSON COUNTY, KENTUCKY

Walking Path: 2.2 miles, hiking trail. Not accessible.

Features: Pristine woodland walk. Rock formations, creek ravines, gravel and sand "beach" along a wide stretch of Harrods Creek.

Facilities: None.

Getting there: North US 42 to Prospect, Kentucky.
Turn right into the Hunting Creek subdivision on Hunting Creek Drive. At the traffic circle, continue onto Deep Creek Drive. Turn left on Montero Drive. The park's trailhead is on the right. Park on Montero Drive near the trailhead.

http://prospectky.us/services/parks-and-recreation/

*"Cicadas chirred high above us in the tall tree canopy as we entered the
dense woodland and found cooling breezes."*

This park, nestled deep in an eastern Jefferson County, Kentucky subdivision, comprises 105 acres and has about four miles of trails offering hiking ranging from easy to moderate. The park winds along tranquil areas of Harrods Creek; its wildlife and varied eco-system include anything from wild turkey to white-tailed deer. In fact, we saw a number of deer on our walk in late September. While not the most senior-friendly walking area (we recommend good physical condition, sturdy hiking boots and a walking cane), we had to include this unique walk because of the outstanding nature excursion it offers, literally in the backyard of some suburban dwellings.

This is a new park (opened in 2012), which offers a pristine old-growth forest walking experience. Residents and volunteers spearheaded the effort to open up this beautiful nature area to public access. On the day of our visit, we encountered several groups of hikers, including kids, adults, and older folks too. Seems word of mouth has spread quickly about this wonderful natural park and trail area.

After parking along the road, we got out and immediately went to read the trailhead sign for information about the trails. We decided to follow the blue trail, which offers a 2. 2-mile round trip with a unique destination point, the "beach." We were glad to immediately get into the deeply shaded woods on this very warm and muggy day. As always, we recommend carrying plenty of water and applying bug spray prior to hiking.

The trail started out a bit tricky, navigating a descending set of flat rock steps down to a stream valley. Water trickling in the stream to the left sounded refreshing on this hot summer afternoon. We were glad we had doused ourselves in bug spray before beginning our walk, as the mosquitos were definitely at home here. Cicadas chirred high above us in the tall tree canopy as we entered the dense woodland and found cooling breezes.

On this outing, our just-turned-12-year-old had brought her "trick or treat" bag with her to collect her nature finds. She is an eagle-eyed collector of all things interesting in woodlands—rocks, shells, fossils, driftwood, acorns, sweet gum pods, hickory nuts, hedge apples and whatever else looks intriguing.

Watch on your left for a dramatic creek drop about a tenth of a mile in. It will make a pretty waterfall after a good rain. On this day, though, it only offered a trickle.

The trail crosses the creek and then offers another set of rustic stone steps leading upward. I love the combination of water, woods, and stone steps. It always feels like a fairy forest to me when I see stone work in the woods. The creek crossing here is a great place for kids to poke a stick around in the water, and that's just what our daughter had to do before we could continue. She made a "nature cupcake"— with an acorn top above a lump of mud.

We could have done without the noise—and unfortunately the smell too—of a nearby water treatment facility. However, it was short lived as we trekked a bit further along the snaking path into a pristine open woodland, enjoying some very large and soaring old-growth trees. We felt glad that we did not notice any dead ash trees—as the emerald ash borer has decimated many of these old-growth trees in the Indiana area where we live.

The next feature we came to on the trail was a log-and-plank bridge followed by a well-placed bench. We noted again the trickling stream rivulets all along the trail. We enjoyed resting on this bench and gazing out at the restful deep green woodland. We knew it would only be a matter of weeks before the lush greens turned to the golds, reds, oranges, and yellows of fall.

Note the lush ferns that pop up under roots of large trees near this bench. Also be sure to look up at the shagbark tree beside the bench. What caused it to curve its trunk so high up? After a leisurely rest, we continued on.

A fork in the trail leading to the orange trail was closed due to construction at the time of this writing. When the orange trail is complete, it will offer a path looping back to the trailhead. For now, we were content to walk in and out on the blue trail.

We came to another log-and-plank bridge and crossed over into a more dense and overgrown area of the trail. It was deeply shaded and quiet. We noticed the insects and birdsong. Suddenly, our daughter yelled, "Look! Tiny snake!" We hurried to try to catch a glimpse, but alas, the small snake had quickly slithered into the dense flora. We lamented that as adults we are not as observant as a child who is continually scanning the ground—and closer to it than we are.

I relaxed into the rhythm of my own walking steps, as I am always pleased to do on these nature outings. It was an easy walk so far. I love the almost meditative state I can enter on a stroll through the woods. A small voice from behind interrupted my reverie. "Are we still going to get froyo when we are done?"

Ah, there is only so much peaceful nature a youngster can take before the lure of the civilized world returns. Yes, we will get an ice cream treat when we are through, I called to her. Even I was looking forward to something frozen after this very muggy walk.

But back to nature. We were now entering a patch of thick brush where the trail narrowed. We passed a meadow to the right that reminded our daughter of the Hunger Games. Wait, what? "The meadow reminds me of the cornucopia in the movie." Sigh. You would probably need to be a teenager, or close to it, to understand. She is growing up way too fast, I thought.

We climbed a small hill to yet another log bridge and passed several large moss-covered boulders. We were now entering a different ecosystem. Steep rocky walls on the north side of the trail provided the answer for where the boulders had come from. We were entering the Harrods Creek valley. The rock walls provided welcome cooling breezes as we descended to the creek bottom. The wide, blue-green water of Harrods Creek came into view as the cliff walls ended. We could hear rushing water ahead.

The trail is rocky as it nears the creek. The path emerges across a grassy swath and the "beach" comes into view. We had finally reached our destination point. It is a small but lovely gravelly sand embankment that provides access to the water. Our 12-year-old immediately poked her stick into the sand to pick out small mollusk shells. She found some very large ones as well, and delighted in making a "nature sub sandwich" out of two of them.

You will want to allow some time to enjoy this lovely spot. The creek is wide and lively here and we enjoyed the sound of the rushing water. It splits in front of the beach into two streams on either side of a marsh area. On the north side of the beach, the water is quieter and schools of small fish can be observed swimming around.

Each of us in our hiking group drifted into our own worlds as we explored the water, sand, shells, and rocks. I marveled at how close nature always is, and yet how we seem to lose sight of it each day as we go about the bustle of our busy lives. I thought, as I often do on these nature walks, how these outings with my family are so "life-giving" (one of my favorite words), offering us a respite from the stresses of our work week.

"Plop!" A large splash in the stream interrupted my thoughts. The girl had thrown a large rock out into the middle of the creek. She laughed at her success. The splash brought her dad around and a rock skipping competition ensued. "Get lower," her dad suggested when her rocks would not skip. The coaching worked as her next rock hopped several times across the stream. Success! She beamed.

I sat for a bit more in the warm sun, enjoying their banter and the beauty and peace of this nature outing. The summer sun glinted across the quickly moving water and I let it lull me into resting my eyes a bit. We enjoyed our relaxing break at our hike's destination until the sun began to set behind the trees, then reluctantly headed back to the blue trail for our return trip.

On our return walk, we were rewarded by the sight of several large deer bounding along the trail near the rocky cliff bottoms. Other hikers we passed told us there were seven more deer ahead. We saw a few more as we left the park.

A few notes for this outing: Be sure to pack in some water bottles for this walk. We also suggest taking a snack to eat at the beach. You'll want to linger there for a while. One additional note: we actually heard a fellow hiker's cell phone ring on this walk. It was very distracting. We would say to always carry your phone, but please put it on silent for your walk.

We were all looking forward to ice cream after our exertion on this warm summer day. We recalled a frozen yogurt shop in one of the shopping centers along US 42 and eagerly looked forward to a visit. Alas, we learned it had gone out of business. We opted for Blizzards and a smoothie at the Dairy Queen on US 42 on our way home. We can always count on a delicious treat at DQ when a local ice cream shop can't be found. And for those like me who are watching their sugar or fat intake, we suggest a delicious small fruit smoothie with protein boost from DQ.

Again, while this outing is not a paved walk and is definitely a bit more challenging than most of the other walks in this guide, we included it as a short hike into a pristine nature area nestled in the backyards of suburban dwellers. We passed a number of older adults on the trip including several sets of multi-generation families. For those with no physical handicaps, this trail can be enjoyed if one just takes it slow and treks carefully. It is a very rewarding excursion that feels a million miles away.

HAYSWOOD NATURE RESERVE INDIAN CREEK TRAIL

HARRISON COUNTY, INDIANA

Walking Path: Two miles, paved, completely accessible.

Features: Repurposed Pratt truss-design bridge over wide Indian Creek, meadowlands and forests.

Facilities: Rustic restroom facilities in picnic areas.

Getting there: South of Corydon, Indiana, at 755 State Road 135—approximately 30 minutes west of Louisville on I-64.

http://www.harrisoncoparks.com/HNR. html

We featured Hayswood Nature Reserve in our last book, *Take A Hike, Louisville!*, with a high-elevation rugged walk to the top of a cliff overlooking the town of Corydon. That nature hike winds into the wild natural area to a spectacular view. That spectacular climb is not our destination for today.

In 2011, a new paved walking path was opened in another area of the park. The walkway is part of a larger trail called Indian Creek Trail that, when completed, will be a two-mile paved walking trail winding down into the town of Corydon. The walk we will describe is a two-mile round trip traveling along and over Indian Creek, featuring a beautifully repurposed bridge called the Rothrock Mill Bridge. It spans Indian Creek, at about a half mile into the trail.

Once you pull into the reserve park, which is off to the left on State Road 135,

"One gets a sense of peace from the bridge itself, almost as if it breathes a sigh of contentment that it is now providing services to pedestrians savoring nature."

follow the road to the end of the reserve. You will go around the scenic picnic area to the bottom of the hill. Park near the fishing lake and look for the trailhead near Indian Creek. You'll see the tall highway bridge to the west, high overhead above the creek.

This trail is completely accessible, paved, and plenty wide for multiuse. No motor vehicles, alcohol, or firearms are allowed. Pets are allowed on a leash, with waste removal.

The path skirts along an expansive meadow, which is the scene of an annual July Civil War reenactment of General John Hunt Morgan's Raid on Corydon. It is an impressive reenactment with horses, cannons, marching brigades, and creekside encampments. It is well worth a visit in July if you can make it! But on our late summer evening walk, all was quiet on the battlefield as we began our trek. We could almost hear the mosquitos buzzing down by the creek.

As you begin walking, you will notice the surrounding forested knobs rising above Indian Creek. This night, it was hot and still, with a bit of cloud cover and a small threat of rain. We hoped to get our walk in before any summer pop-up storm could thwart us.

The feel of rain was somewhat confirmed as we looked down toward the creek and saw that the ducks were standing in the shallow water with their heads tucked in, as if expecting a storm. We hurried along the paved path, anxious to see the restored Rothrock Mill Bridge over Indian Creek. We had been on this walk once before, two years earlier, after the bridge had first opened along the path. We were anxious to view it again, remembering it to be an impressive sight, and to walk along the now-paved path continuing on after crossing the bridge.

The woods were still as we walked, dotted by bright yellow, white, and purple wildflowers along the creek bank. We thought that the forested uplands surrounding us as we walked would be really beautiful decked out in all their splendid fall colors. A return visit in the fall proved us a bit wrong about that, however, as the colors were very muted—yellows and browns, but no bright reds or golds.

There are large rocks along the path that are just perfect for your kids to climb on. They are not so high that they can't jump off safely and our youngster made sure to test out each and every one. Benches are also strategically placed to rest and enjoy the creek views. We did not rest though, as we really wanted to get this walk in before rain.

There are several dirt paths that lead down to the creek, and nice places at the bottom to view the creek. Watch for snakes, however, as poisonous ones have been spotted in the park. Fishing is also allowed in the creek; a passerby mentioned that one can catch catfish and bass in the creek.

Continuing along, note the natural prairie field on the left. A sign alerts park maintenance not to mow or spray this area. It is a nice view as you begin the ascent to the bridge.

The ramp up to the bridge begins about a half-mile into the trail. It is an impressive ramp, built up with stone supports. A sign alerts trail users that a sharp turn right is ahead. As you start to climb the ramp, you cannot see the bridge.

As soon as you turn the corner, the surprising and impressive sight of the bridge comes into view. It is breathtaking. The Rothrock Bridge, repurposed for this trail, was originally built in 1915 and provided a crossing over the Blue River, connecting Harrison and Crawford counties for 90 years. Signage at the site explains that it is a Pratt through-truss bridge which includes vertical members and diagonals that slope down toward the center of the bridge. It is very pretty, and was once a common configuration in truss bridges. The Rothrock Bridge was replaced in 2005, and in 2010, it was carefully disassembled and moved to its new location on the Indian Creek Trail. It was reassembled, cleaned, painted, and updated with new decking and handrails. There are only three remaining steel truss bridges in Harrison County; only one carries vehicles.

As you walk up to the bridge, you'll want your camera, and you'll want to spend time on the bridge getting good views from both sides of the bridge. In the middle of the bridge are fabulous views of the wide Indian Creek below and the surrounding forest. It was, for us, reminiscent of some of the trails in the Great Smoky Mountains. The creek below is clear and usually lively. Tonight, it was barely flowing, but we could still see small fish even from high above on the bridge.

We loved walking on the restored wood planks of the bridge and leaning over the railings to view the creek. One gets a sense of peace and happiness from the bridge itself, almost as if it breathes a sigh of contentment that it is now providing services to pedestrians savoring nature. It seems glad not to know the jarring noise of vehicular traffic any longer, yet remain integrally purposeful to the Indian Creek Trail, continuing a useful life into its retirement.

After the bridge, the paved walk continues on for another half mile. If you are able to continue, we highly advise walking until the path ends in a stop sign. This next section is a nature wonder, winding through dense and shady woodlands with old-growth trees. The path is pleasingly winding and runs along Indian Creek, now on your left, after you cross over the bridge.

About a quarter-mile later, we were amazed to see an arched tree bent over completely but still alive. We knew it was alive as we observed lots of small, leafed-out offshoot branches. This is a low-lying area, prone to flooding, as evidenced by the many coppiced trees.

This path is a perfect nature lover's walk with dense woods, a lively and wide creek and prairie-like meadows. The entire walkway is paved and accessible, offering a total distance of two miles. Plans are in place to continue the paved path, connecting it to another path leading down to the Harrison County YMCA. But for us, just this much of the completed walk suited us perfectly on this crackling, rain-threatening summer evening.

Our daughter was in ice cream mode now, as we headed back along the trail and to our car. It was getting to be past dinnertime, and more folks had arrived to walk the path after dinner and before the rain. On this night were mostly families with kids and several walking baby strollers, plus many folks with pets on leashes. We slowed just a bit on the way back, along the rocky edge of the trail, to observe a tiny dragonfly and a small jumping toad. We shooed them both off the path into the undergrowth, satisfied they would be safely off the trail and out of harm's way.

We were beginning to sense that it was time for that refreshing lure of our ice cream treat. We headed back into Corydon to the Shireman's Farm Market and fresh peach ice cream. The locals all know this popular spot at the corner of Highway 135 and Old State Road 135. You may have passed it on your way in— every year a large sign across its roof screams, "Fresh Peach Ice Cream." You can't miss it if you are visiting in season. They also have pumpkin ice cream for later in the fall. It is soft serve with fresh peach flavor and real bits of peaches. Yum—perfect on a summer evening. After enjoying our ice cream treat and purchasing a basket of homegrown tomatoes, we headed home, happy to have gotten our outing in before the summer rainstorm.

KULMER BEACH RESERVE

JEFFERSON COUNTY, KENTUCKY

Walking Path: 1.7 miles, gravel trail and beach walk.

Features: Picnic pavilion and beach along the river. You will hike along an old overgrown jeep road and descend to the oldest beach in Louisville. We recommend wearing sturdy shoes or hiking boots due to the uneven surfaces and beach debris.

Facilities: None.

Getting there: Off Dixie Highway in Southwest Jefferson County, one mile north of West Point, Kentucky. Turn onto Abbott's Beach Road. Drive past several homes on the river. Kulmer Reserve is straight ahead. Parking lot on the left; picnic pavilion on the right overlooking the Ohio River.

http://www.louisvilleky.gov/MetroParks/parks/kulmer/

We had first heard about the Kulmer Reserve and beach several years ago but until this day had not been able to dedicate an afternoon for a visit. We were very interested to find the place, as we had been told it was a wild and scenic area. Wild and scenic within the city limits of Louisville? We thought it would be a unique area to explore, and we were not disappointed. I will backtrack here for a minute and let readers know that since our visit, some research turned up the interesting history of Kulmer Beach. Contrary to our initial impressions, it was, in fact, not a natural feature. In fact, this beach was the first developed beach in Louisville back in 1920, according to the Encyclopedia of Louisville. Other beaches that were developed in the early 1900s include Transylvania, Turner's, and Shawnee. Swimming beaches and swimming in the Ohio River were popular summer recreational outlets until about the 1960s, when most beaches added clubs and swimming pools, and pollution in the river made swimming in it a thing of the past. Since this particular beach

"We realized we could actually take a long walk along a beach—in the middle of landlocked Louisville, Kentucky."

was seemingly abandoned after its heyday and subsequently turned into a nature reserve, we were even more excited to find it and take a walk along it if possible.

We arrived to explore this somewhat hidden park on a chilly and windy, but sunny early fall afternoon. Information online says it is located on Kulmer Beach Road, but our GPS could not find it. We happened to spot a small green directional sign for Kulmer Reserve along Dixie Highway and turned onto Abbott's Beach Road, then veered left, guessing we were headed in the correct direction. After driving for a block or two, we saw another sign for the reserve and pulled forward into a small parking area.

We exited our car and walked across the road toward a rundown picnic pavilion. It was in a state of some disrepair and the views overlooking the river were blocked by the still-leafed out trees which were just starting to turn colors for the fall. In the wooded area on the backside of the pavilion, we found a narrow trail descending to a small, steep set of concrete steps and realized that this may once have been a main path leading down to the beach. We decided to continue and found that indeed this trail did lead to the beach, but it was overgrown and hard to follow. We found a better path to the beach, and the following alternative is the way we would recommend.

To get the beach, we found that all you have to do is follow the road you entered the reserve on—Abbott's/Kulmer Beach road. It was gated the day we visited, but walkers can go around the gate on foot. It becomes a somewhat overgrown jeep road, but is fairly easy to discern. Walking along the road, you will be next to the railroad and will pass two huge old-growth oak trees. The path branches off toward the river to the right; continuing straight, it becomes overgrown. Take the path to the right to go down to the beach area.

We were anxious to view the old beach and were not disappointed as it came into view through the woods. "Wow," we breathed as a wide, sandy beach spread out in front of us. We were not expecting to see a real, sandy beach along the Ohio River. A pebbly cul-de-sac area for fishing perhaps, but not an actual wide and sandy beach.

We tried to remember if we had ever come across something like this in all of our local nature explorations but couldn't come up with anything quite like it. We had certainly been to lakes with small developed swimming beaches, but nothing like this long and wide beach that stretched in both directions as far as we could see. We realized that we could actually take a long walk along a beach -- in the middle of landlocked Louisville, Kentucky.

Once we got over our stunned surprise, we began walking along the beach and exploring this unusual nature feature—at least very unusual for our area.

On our visit this day, the weather was chilly with a stiff wind whipping up river waves breaking along the shore. A barge churned by, kicking up the waves even higher. We walked north along the deserted beach populated only with tall tufts of beach grass. The wind and sounds of the surf felt ocean-like. I swear I could smell salty air.

Children on this excursion will love collecting rocks, stones, driftwood and shells along the shore. Our 12-year-old had her handy "nature trick or treat bag" with her to pick up interesting objects.

This is a wild and scenic area very few people seem to know about. It could, however, really use some good volunteer help in cleaning it up. Drift trash and tires are strewn along the beach, though it did not distract too much in our enjoyment of discovering this place and the feeling that it was remote and lost in time.

I enjoyed resting on a rock and listening to the surprising sounds of waves rushing in and breaking on the beach. The air and river seemed fresher and cleaner here than near the downtown area, even with the Louisville Gas and Electric power plant spewing out smoke in the distance.

Wind, sand, surf, and rocks—what more could one ask for in landlocked Jefferson County? The only other nature experience that comes close to this, in our opinion, is the falls of the Ohio, which can, depending on the weather, also provide the experience of being near an ocean. I marveled that such a wild natural resource would be so close—just over an embankment from a major highway and right there—all but hidden from the world.

Our daughter had grabbed a stick to draw in the sand and scratched out the symbol # and the letter I. I said, "Oh you wrote Hi."

Her dad said to her: "You want to play tic-tac-toe?"

She said, "Uh no, that's hashtag, I—as in me." Sigh. It's hard to get them away from their technology, but at least she was tweeting on a beach, not a cellphone.

After walking up and down both directions of the beach and enjoying the brisk but sunny afternoon out strolling along the river's edge, we returned to the wide path and headed back up to our car, leaving the wild and windy sand and surf behind. At the picnic shelter, the wind was calmer, and the air warmer. What a difference! The warmth of the sun provided the only motivation needed to find an ice cream treat after our walk.

We found a wonderful place for a treat just up the highway in West Point, Kentucky. The Star Café is located inside the old West Point Hotel, which is listed on the National Register of Historic Places. You may even want to save your appetite for a great home-cooked meal here instead of opting for just a sweet treat.

To reach the Cafe, turn right onto Highway 31W (Dixie Highway) after leaving the reserve. Drive 1.4 miles to West Point and turn right on Lillie Lewis Way. The West Point Hotel is on the right, and the Star Café is inside. They will be happy to pack you up an ice cream sundae, brownie sundae, or a piece of homemade German chocolate cake with ice cream or other delectable desserts of the day. We took our treats out to the front porch and enjoyed them in the comfy porch swing and rockers. Please note that as of this writing, the café is not open on Mondays, Tuesdays, or Wednesdays, so you may want to check before you visit.

The Kulmer Beach Reserve is a completely unique, out-of-the-way nature walk that will make for a perfect afternoon excursion—especially with a visit to the Star Café afterward. We were delighted that we had finally found the abandoned beach—you will be too.

O'BANNON WOODS STATE PARK - TULIP VALLEY TRAIL

HARRISON COUNTY, INDIANA

Walking Path: One mile, compacted gravel and boardwalks.

Features: Walk through deep woodlands with old-growth trees and wildlife viewing areas.

Facilities: Restrooms available at nature center near trailhead.

Getting there: From Louisville, head west on I-64, continue to the Corydon exit (Exit 105). At the exit, go south on S.R.135 to S.R.62. Go west on S.R.62 about 10 miles. Go south on S.R.462 about three miles to the park entrance. Follow the signs to the Hickory Hollow Nature Center. Trailhead is at the end of the parking area.

http://www.in.gov/dnr/parklake/2976.htm

An earlier summer visit to this park led us by accident to this wonderful trail. We had come for a picnic and swimming and decided to take a side visit to the nature center. We discovered that there is a lot to love at this Indiana state park (formerly Wyandotte Woods State Recreation Area), developed in the 1930s by one of the few African American Civilian Conservation Corp units. Indiana's first natural and scenic river, Blue River, flows through it. Today, the park offers 3,000 acres of recreational opportunities including biking, hiking, camping, caves, fishing, horseback riding, aquatic swimming pool, picnic shelters, nature center, and a pioneer farmstead. It's well worth a visit and we were looking forward to exploring Indiana's newest state park on a warm early fall afternoon.

We usually find our way to the nature center of any state park we visit as a

"As soon as you enter, you are transported to another world."

starting point, and today was no exception. The Hickory Hollow Nature Center offers the traditional interpretive nature activities such as a bird blind, interpretive programs, and live reptiles and amphibians. The property near the nature center also has a pioneer farmstead with a uniquely restored, working antique hay press barn, complete with two live oxen for power. The hay press is a huge, three-story stationary hay baling mechanism constructed in 1849 in Crawford County. It is one of a very few remaining working hay presses, many of which had been located along the Ohio River in the last half of the 19th century. This one was donated to the Indiana Department of Natural Resources in 2000 and moved to the park, where the barn was reconstructed for its housing. The hay press was made operational for public demonstrations, which continue today.

We enjoyed exploring the nature center first, especially the wildlife blind, where we looked out upon a wild turkey feeding station and were rewarded when one huge turkey showed up for a snack. We were told he is a regular visitor and comes as soon as feed is put out. We also enjoyed learning about the hay press. But we were here for a walk, so we headed outside to find the trailhead for the accessible Tulip Valley Trail, located to the side of the nature center's parking area.

Signage at the trailhead informs hikers that this trail will take you into a unique and educational woodland setting. A crankshaft audio box gives more information about what to expect: sensory gardens, historic sites, mysterious holes, native plantings, and wildlife viewing. We were anxious to get started.

This path is made of compacted gravel. The surface is hard and smooth for the most part, but it is not paved, and in some places there a few ruts, so keep watch. As soon as you enter, you are transported to another world. It is almost startling to be in the dense woods so immediately after leaving the relative civilization near the nature center.

The wind through the tops of the tall trees on the afternoon of our walk was music to my ears. As it always does when I begin walking in nature, my breathing slowed as I inhaled deep breaths of fresh, pungent forest air and enjoyed the restful views of a gracefully curving path and tall, green-topped trees.

The trail twists this way and that, winding through peaceful woodland growth of old trees. Signs are in regular intervals at the base of those trees. Some we observed: yellow poplar, pignut hickory, white ash, Mockernut hickory, and sycamore. Lots of hickory trees, we thought; no wonder the nature center is named Hickory Hollow.

There are plenty of benches along the trail to rest after climbing the gentle inclines. Interpretive signs along the way highlight other features. We were alerted to look for some of those mysterious holes mentioned earlier, and could not fathom what might have caused them.

We continued walking on the warm fall afternoon, rewarded by dappled sunlight and cool breezes. We walked slowly and took in the sight of many large old trees. Some had triple trunks with wide circumferences and soared toward the sky.

Bridges carry you over small ravines, and rustic stones line the path in some areas. I observed a leaf, caught in a spider web just off the trail, seemingly dancing in midair. Well, that's perfect for fall and the coming of Halloween, I thought.

We came next upon the historic site, but not much was visible with the summer overgrowth. A sign and audio box informed us that we were standing at Lynch Homestead. Some remnants here include the foundation of an old schoolhouse, old plantings such as yucca plants, and twin chimneys, which were not visible. Perhaps a wintertime walk might reveal these remains of a bygone time.

A sign after the historic site is strategically located next to a shagbark hickory tree, where, if you look up, you might see some roosting bats. Seems they like to shelter under this tree's loose bark—very interesting, but I did not want to disturb any of those creatures! The Shagbark tree is interesting too—with its dripping pieces of bark, it is exactly as its name describes, and seems to be the perfect home for bats.

The trail leads to a series of boardwalks which are quite nicely built and interesting to walk over. Some are curved into U shapes, and others are elevated four to six feet off the ground, giving a feeling of walking in the lower tree canopy.

A small pond is off to one side of the trail. We could hear a woodpecker and locusts in the distance. Our younger walking companions observed a deer at the pond's edge, dipping its head for a drink. At the sound of the hikers, the deer raised its head, turned, and leaped off away from the pond.

The wildlife viewing area, next along the trail, consists of a two-story blind that you can climb up in and look out several window cutouts onto a cleared meadow, surrounded by the woods. The blind is painted camouflage, and on this day, we were graced with viewing a gang of wild turkeys out in the field.

After the wildlife blind, the path winds down a gentle decline back to the nature center. Having walked a one-mile loop, you will end up at the back of the pioneer homestead. Plan to spend a little extra time exploring the rustic structures, including a mortise-and-tenon barn, and be sure to check out the huge live oxen in their pen before leaving.

We loved this beautiful trail—not only for the lovely nature it offers, but also for the way the trail is constructed with the unique boardwalks and wildlife viewing area, and for its accessibility.

Although we fervently wished we had more time to remain in this rustic park, alas, we had to head back into town. But not before getting our ice cream treat, of course.

For the best ice cream the nearby town of Corydon has to offer, head out of the park the way you came in and continue on to Corydon. Stay on Highway 62 until you reach the center of town, where you will be on Walnut Street. Look for Emery's Ice Cream on the left and pull into the parking lot.

Emery's is a local favorite and an old-fashioned ice cream soda fountain. It offers many freshly prepared ice cream flavors, including seasonal favorites such as blackberry cobbler ice cream and pumpkin ice cream. They also have sundaes, malts, floats, splits, and a huge selection of candies. Our 11-year-old loved her cup of Crazy Cookie Dough ice cream.

After filling up on the homemade ice cream, we were ready to head back home on a lovely Sunday afternoon.

OHIO RIVER GREENWAY -
NEW ALBANY AT RIVERFRONT PARK

FLOYD COUNTY, INDIANA

Walking Path: Approximately one mile,
paved, completely accessible.

Features: Ohio River access and views.

Facilities: Restroom building near the amphitheater.
Open seasonally.

Getting there: I-64 to Exit 123/New Albany/Elm Street. Turn right
on State Street. Third left (Ohio River Scenic Byway/Main Street).
Right on Sixth Street. Continue to E. Water Street.
There are several parking lots along the Greenway, park
and playground, and amphitheater.

http://www.ohiorivergreenway.org/

According to the Ohio River Greenway website, the mission of the greenway is to "provide a common linkage between the Communities of Jeffersonville, Clarksville, and New Albany, Indiana, along the banks of the Ohio River and to promote a passive recreational environment for river access, while allowing each community to construct riverfront amenities to enhance the overall project." The organization is well on its way to meeting its goal. We certainly appreciate the parts of the paved greenway that allow a relaxing walk along the banks of the Ohio River. This stretch in the New Albany area makes for a wonderful afternoon or evening walk, and is especially scenic when clear skies allow for a pretty sunset behind the Sherman Minton Bridge. There are other completed sections of the greenway in Clarksville and Jeffersonville, but this stretch in New Albany allows pedestrians to

"On a chilly afternoon, I headed to the Greenway to walk after a particularly busy workday."

walk closer to the river itself.

On a chilly but sunny November afternoon, I headed to the greenway to walk after a particularly busy work day. I drove down Main Street in New Albany and turned onto E. Water Street, entering the park to the right. I drove past a very nice playground, and parked along the river near the yellow-canopied New Albany amphitheater before heading across the roadway to the greenway. I walked west toward the striking Sherman Minton Bridge.

The river's waters were deep blue and a bit lively on this brisk afternoon. Cars and trucks zipped by on the bridge ahead. I was grateful to be peacefully de-stressing along the Greenway in the open air—and not in a car on the Sherman Minton.

Viewing the river at this location is calming because on each side is green space—dense woods on the Louisville side, and parkland on the Indiana side. As I walked, the sun became a bright, peachy orange ball dipping down below the bridge. I loved gazing out at the expansive river and just walked slowly, breathing in the fresh air and detoxing my mind on this late fall afternoon.

I noted there are not many options for picnicking for those who might like to take this walk with children or a larger group on a warmer day. The amphitheater has grassy areas for spreading a blanket, however, and the kiddos will love the nearby playground.

After passing under the bridge, you will simply turn around and walk in the other direction. The greenway continues for about 1.5 miles toward 9th Street in New Albany. It links up with the Loop Island Wetlands area in New Albany. If you choose to continue into this area, watch little ones carefully, especially at the old railroad trestle. The greenway will eventually continue through this area.

This walk is also perfect in the summer as it provides close river access and cooling breezes. After walking on a warm afternoon or evening, the perfect option for an ice cream treat is the Comfy Cow at 109 East Market in New Albany. You can walk to it from the greenway if you'd like. From the parking area on Water Street, walk over the levee at the amphitheater and down the steps. You will see the Floyd

County YMCA to the left. Walk two blocks up State Street to East Market, where you will see Comfy Cow on the corner of State and Market.

Comfy Cow is a wonderful local ice cream and confection shop. They offer seasonal, hand-dipped premium ice cream flavors in cones, cups, and sundaes. You can also get a slice of ice cream pie, a smoothie or even a Pooch Pop for your dog. Since I was walking on a chilly evening, I decided against ice cream and headed up State Street in New Albany to Starbucks for a Pumpkin Spice Latte instead. A perfect sweet treat to warm up after a chilly but invigorating walk. I felt great after my brisk walk, and with coffee in hand, headed home in a much improved and relaxed frame of mind. Ahh, the benefits of a nature walk never fail to improve one's mental state and outlook on life—and a little caffeine added the perfect pick-me-up.

OHIO RIVER GREENWAY
CLARKSVILLE AT FALLS OF THE OHIO

CLARK COUNTY, INDIANA

Walking Path: One to two miles, paved, completely accessible.

Features: Ohio River access and scenic views of falls of the Ohio and the Louisville skyline.

Facilities: Restroom building near the playground. Open seasonally.

Getting there: I-65 North from Louisville to Exit 0. Turn left on Court Avenue. Right on US 31 S. Left on Missouri Avenue. Right on West Market. Continue to Ohio River Scenic Byway. Park on the left, across from the Widow's Walk Ice Creamery.

http://www.ohiorivergreenway.org/

Here is another section of the Ohio River Greenway to explore—this time from the Clarksville side. This walk is great any time of the year but is especially great in the summertime. It is completely accessible and packs in many unique features in a short walk, including very scenic nature views, a beautiful Louisville skyline view, wonderful information signage along the path, and a great ice cream stand on the premises.

Park on the left across from the Widow's Walk Ice Creamery (which is where you will end up at the end of your walk), then head over to the river side. Stop for a minute to read the information kiosk about the "Scenic Spans" of the historic Louisville bridges. Interesting tidbits ("By the Ways") include the fact that one nearby bridge, the Big Four Railroad Bridge, was once the longest iron bridge in the nation. It is now a converted pedestrian bridge, offering a fabulous walking

"It packs in many unique features in a short walk."

experience (See "Big Four Bridge" walk in this book).

Continue along the Ohio River Greenway, which is the paved path with a painted middle line. The greenway runs along the parkland. You will pass several pretty benches that overlook the river and a nice playground and picnic area where you will see the restroom building. Read another sign along the path to find out more about how the land in this area was once under a tropical sea. Another sign has a photo of how the falls of the Ohio looked before the locks and dam were modernized in the 1960s.

The walk is elevated above the river along a high bank, with open river views. As you approach the railroad bridge, you will see how the dam operates to divert the water into the locks and away from the falls. On the falls side, the river is usually rushing with water pouring over the falls. It always seems very impressive. Continue toward the Falls of the Ohio Interpretative Center, a unique building that blends into its natural surroundings with a sedimentary, layered-rock façade.

The greenway crosses the road and continues up a moderate hill to provide a great view of the falls of the Ohio below. From this vantage point, one can see the river at the falls, the interpretative center building, and the statue of Meriwether Lewis and George Rogers Clark, the two explorers of the Corps of Discovery expedition which opened up the American West. This is the point where the expedition started!

At the top of the hill, come to a stop sign and make a decision. Either continue on the greenway for an elevated walk along the levee, or turn back and retrace your steps back to your car. You have walked about a half mile. If you turn back at this point, you will walk a total of one mile. You can lengthen your walk by continuing a bit before turning back. You may also choose to return along the sidewalk across the road once you return to the park. This side of the road provides shade from the large trees along the high river bank.

On the slightly chilly but sunny fall afternoon of my visit, I chose to turn back at the stop sign. I enjoyed a leisurely walk back and especially loved the views of the

"This is the point where the expedition started."

Louisville skyline from this vantage point across the river.

I eyed the Widow's Walk Ice Creamery, near the parking area at the start of the greenway, considering whether the day was too chilly for some ice cream (the outlet also rents bicycles out of this location in season). Unfortunately, I could not get ice cream because the popular place is only open seasonally. Darn! Fortunately, the Orange Clover Kitchen, located at 590 Missouri Avenue, just up the road a bit toward the Clark Memorial Bridge (Second Street Bridge), is open for breakfast and lunch, and has a nice selection of sweet treats.

Nature, scenery, a lovely skyline, unique information kiosks, playground and picnic tables, and an ice cream outlet open in the summertime in a perfect location at the end of your path make this walk just about perfect. Enjoy!

PERRIN FAMILY PARK

CLARK COUNTY, INDIANA

Walking Path: 1.25 miles, paved.

Features: Scenic lake with waterfowl feeding station, woodlands, meadows, bird watching, teddy bear museum.

Note: There is a NO PETS policy in this park.

Facilities: Restroom building at entrance to paved walking path.

Getting there: From Louisville, take I-65 North to Jeffersonville, Indiana, and Exit 0/Court Avenue. Take a left on Graham Street, then right on Eighth Street. Drive 2.5 miles and take a right on Perrin Lane. Park entrance is on the left.

www.perrinfamilypark.org

This lovely, family-owned nature park in Jeffersonville, Indiana, opened to the public in 1991. It is a truly hidden gem that the general public (especially on the Louisville side of the Ohio River) probably hasn't heard of. People from Jeffersonville are aware of this nature treasure, however, and I was fortunate to find out about it from one of the local residents who told me about it upon hearing of my interest in nature walks.

The park is located in the heart of Jeffersonville across from the local aquatic center. I had noted the trees and green space in the area when visiting the pool several times, but was not aware of the nature preserve within its fences. The property was actually first owned by George Rogers Clark. H.L. and Catherine Perrin purchased the land in 1943 and maintained a dairy farm on the property for 31 years before donating it for a nature preserve, managed by a private foundation.

"The feeding station is surrounded by trees and a large weeping willow, providing shade and shelter for some of the waterfowl."

According to the website, the goal of Perrin Family Park is to provide the community with a unique mix of educational and recreational opportunities. The park includes a 1.25-mile paved walking path which circles a lake and waterfowl feeding station before meandering through trees and meadows. There is also a lovely, shaded picnic area with two shelter houses, a full-acre playground with large sandboxes and even a teddy bear museum (more about that later). We were looking forward to visiting this unique park, right in our own Indiana backyard.

Upon entering the park, pull straight in and park in the parking lot. A statue of St. Francis greets you; his marker claims that he is the patron saint of ecology and serves as guardian of Perrin Park. You will see the lake ahead. You will notice immediately the quiet provided by a dense line of pine trees surrounding the park and substantially blocking the traffic noise.

Our first visit to this unique park was on a sweltering August afternoon. I love the first moments of exploring a new park. As soon as I step out of the car and view the nature scene around me, my breath slows and my nerves calm. On this hot and muggy day, we were hoping for shade and cool lake breezes and were grateful to find them here.

As soon as we arrived, we were greeted by several flocks of geese taking off from the water and circling around us, lifting off to the south. It felt too early to see them leaving for the winter, but perhaps they were getting an early start. We laughed as they began their ascent, nearly bumping into our heads.

Clean restroom facilities and water fountains are to the right at the beginning of the paved nature trail. We took a few moments to enjoy the lake bank and watch the waterfowl before beginning our walk. Signs informed us of two features along the trail: a waterfowl feeding station, and Healthline Fitness Stations. These stations are located along the trail for those inclined to do jumping jacks, toe touches, chin-ups, and the like. We were not, we laughed—walking and enjoying nature is much more to our liking.

Begin the trail near the restrooms—the trail is a loop that will return you to the opposite parking lot. Before we got into a walking rhythm, another building and sign came upon us: Catherine's Teddy Bear Place. If you are visiting during the months of April through October, the museum is open and you can walk right in. It is a delightful surprise, offering history of the land and park, along with a collection of Catherine Perrin's 650+ teddy bears of all sizes arranged in quaint window scenes. It really is an odd and surprising, but thoroughly enjoyable, diversion to stumble upon in this nature park,

But we were here to walk, not gawk, so we made a quick tour of the quirky museum and walked back to the paved path to begin our outing. Next up on the trail is a headstone of Sarah Lloyd Ewing—all that is left of an old cemetery on the property according to the plaque. We stopped and read for a bit more history, but were anxious to get going.

However, it was going to take us a bit longer before we started that walk in earnest, because the next feature was upon us: the waterfowl feeding station. There was much to see and do at this stop.

The feeding station is a boardwalk with wooden benches, surrounded by trees and a large weeping willow, providing shade and shelter for some of the waterfowl. We noticed a duck egg in a hollowed out spot under one of the benches and were careful to avoid it.

A vending machine at the station offers feed for a quarter. We purchased some and proceeded to the wooden fence overlooking the lake. Across the lake, a heron took off to land on the bank near the feeding station. We watched in amazement as he dipped his bill into the shallow water at the lake's edge, picked a fish right out of the water and took off with it. Now that's what I call a nature experience!

Looking down into the murky water, we noticed large turtles coming right up to the station, and sticking their heads up toward us pleadingly. Fish also came up immediately, along with geese and ducks. We tossed the feed, one or two pieces at a time into the water and laughed at the total feeding frenzy. We felt sorry for the slow turtles; the waterfowl simply swam right over them and pushed them out of the way. Many times, turtle heads ducked quickly into their shells to avoid a duck bill going for a piece of feed. It was all very entertaining, but we still had not started walking.

I was anxious to get into a rhythmic walking gait—it's what I come for on these excursions. I left the others to enjoy the feeding station a bit longer and set out to walk. The path continues in a gentle curve around the lake. An overhang of pine branches offers a bit of shade before a long open swath through a meadow. You will head into a longer shady section next; it is a pretty, tree-lined section of the trail. On the day we visited, we certainly appreciated the cool, green shade. Now we were getting into the calm and steady walking gait that I so enjoy. As we walked, we noticed several gravel offshoot paths, which perhaps offer a bit more "nature" experience, but we were happy to stay on the paved trail.

The summer day we walked, an earlier rain had left small pools of water glistening along the path. We meandered through sun and shade about a half mile and then came upon a gazebo. It's a nice spot to rest and snap a few photos of the lake if you have a camera. We took advantage of the rest stop and enjoyed a few cooling lake breezes as we enjoyed a snack and some water.

Back on the trail, there is another meadow to cross. We observed flocks of geese grazing in the grass. Next along the trail is a lovely, wooded arboretum of sorts with each tree identified with a marker at its base. A multitude of varieties of maples, willows, flowering crab trees, fruit and nut trees line the path. I really had no idea there were so many maple varieties: here were Red Japanese, Trident Red, Crimson King, Deborah, Harlequin, Paperbark, Indian Summer, and others. Our 11-year-old was determined to find a tree to sit in, and she was not disappointed. A black locust tree with a large split offered her the perfect place to chill out, write in her notebook (like mother like daughter), and gaze up at the leafy branches.

After this section, we exited the trail on the other side of the lake near the parking lot and returned to our vehicle. Our walk on this day was enjoyable, but hot and sticky; we were ready for the air-conditioned car and an ice cream treat.

Before leaving the park, we drove along the road that took us to the picnic area. It offers a shady ground for cookouts and a large, one-acre pea gravel playground. Our youngster *had* to swing and explore the variety of play equipment before leaving. There was also a large sandbox—altogether a great place to bring the kids or grandkids. A shelter is available to rent as well.

We loved discovering the multitude of nature this park had to offer. The only hazards were a slightly slick (from the rain) walking surface, and avoiding stepping in duck guano along the path. As always, we reminded ourselves of the reason to carry extra shoes, socks and plastic bags to put our dirty shoes in upon returning to our car.

That concluded our visit to Perrin Family Park. We were definitely ready for something cold after our hot outdoor adventure. We found several possibilities for an ice cream treat nearby. Out of the park, turn right on Eighth Street and continue to Allison Lane. Straight through the light on the left is a Dairy Queen. Or turn left at the light onto Allison and you'll find Chillers across from Jeffersonville High School. Continue to the Meijer's shopping center to find Swirlz Frozen Yogurt. There is also a nearby McDonald's. Here are the addresses:

Chillers Microcreamery—2314 Allison Lane
Dairy Queen—3011 Middle Road
Swirlz Frozen Yogurt—2784 Meijer Drive
McDonald's—3000 E 10th Street

We were short on time, so the drive-through at DQ fit the bill; Chillers would be our first choice on the next visit.

We left with happy feelings over discovering this hidden gem in Jeffersonville, perfect for seniors, families, and grandkids. We felt torn between wanting to spread the word and keeping it our little secret.

PUTNEY POND AND WOODLANDS

JEFFERSON COUNTY, KENTUCKY

Walking Path: Approximately .5 mile paved in-and-out walking path; 1+ miles hiking trails.

Features: Paved walking path along scenic pond, woodland nature trails, wetlands.

Facilities: No restrooms

Getting there: US 42 to Prospect, Kentucky. Turn right at The Landings. Look for the Putney Pond and Woodlands sign immediately to the left. Pull into a circle and park your vehicle on the curb.

http://prospectky.us/services/parks-and-recreation/the-parks/ putney-pond-and-the-woodlands/

Putney Pond and Woodlands is located in northeast Jefferson County in the city of Prospect. It is owned by the City of Prospect and maintained as a natural area. This little nature gem is virtually unknown to most Louisville-area folks, except for those who are Prospect residents. We became aware of the area after writing our last hiking book, and then being contacted by the mayor of Prospect informing us of this area, and asking that it be included in any future publications. We were happy to oblige and headed out to look for the scenic pond and nature trails on a perfectly beautiful sunny and slightly chilly fall afternoon.

After finding our way into the area at the Landings off US 42 and parking along the circle, we hopped out of our vehicle to check out the scenic Putney Pond, which was more like a small lake. The first thing we noticed was the inviting paved walking path encircling the pond and wetlands. We wanted to walk along the lane

"We loved discovering this hidden-in-plain-sight scenic gem."

and immediately took off toward it to take a quick stroll.

The pond is surrounded by wetlands and woodlands. On this day, the fall color was still holding on, and we enjoyed a view of golds and oranges in the trees. Walking down this path with a stained wooden fence along its sides felt like a stroll down a country lane. We were just getting our walking rhythm, when alas, it came to an end way too quickly. This lovely little stretch is only about a quarter-mile long. After climbing a small hill, the walking path dead-ends back into US 42. You will need to turn around and head back. We didn't mind, however, as we loved this short walking path and the natural surroundings.

Back at the parking circle, look for the trailhead sign to the left. Walk up a short rise to view some informational brochures and a map of the hiking trail area. We learned that fishing is allowed in the pond and pets are fine on a leash, but no bikes or horses are allowed on the nature trails. We had not been previously aware that there were also hiking trails through the woodlands here, but decided that we had time to explore.

We grabbed our water bottles and eagerly headed into the woods along the Scenic Loop. The trails are not handicap-accessible. However, a short walk into the woodlands and over a rustic bridge will get you to a bench overlooking a small stream and surrounded by tall old-growth trees. It is a perfectly scenic place to sit and contemplate the beauty of nature. We would suggest if you have an older person in your group or one with some accessibility issues, that it might be acceptable to help your person get to the bench, and then allow him or her to sit and wait while the rest of your party explores the woodlands. The trail makes a loop—it won't take your party too long to circle back, but there is a substantial climb, so keep that in mind.

Shortly after heading into the woods, we spotted both a buck and a doe. They gazed at us curiously but were not too skittish, so we were able to snap a few photos of both of them. The doe was especially cute, coquettishly poking her head out from behind a large tree trunk.

We continued up a steep climb on the scenic loop. The woods were a canopy overhead as we walked in dense shade, grateful for the rays of sunlight breaking through the deep woods. We noted some very large old-growth trees soaring skyward.

The trail winds up a ridge before descending down to another wooden bridge near the pond. You may choose to stretch your legs further by following the signs to the wetlands. If not, simply follow the loop and the signs for Putney Pond to retrace your steps back to the start.

We loved discovering this hidden-in-plain-sight scenic gem. The hiking trails are not entirely accessible, but the paved walk around part of the pond and the lovely and well-marked woodland trails, with benches for resting among the glorious natural area, make this well worth a visit for folks of all ages.

For our ice cream treat, we headed out of the parking circle at The Landings and crossed straight over US 42 into the shopping area, where we spied an Orange Leaf Premium Frozen Yogurt shop and also a Starbucks next door. The youngsters enjoyed some frozen yogurt, while I was thrilled to gulp down a caffeinated drink to boost my energy on this active outdoor afternoon.

RED ORCHARD PARK

SHELBY COUNTY, KENTUCKY

Walking Path: 2.5 miles, mowed grass and gravel.

Features: Expansive hilly views, meadows, creek, orchards, and nature-themed play areas with adult exercise equipment. There is also a dog run area.

Facilities: Restroom building near entrance.

Getting there: The park is located at 704 Kentucky Street, Shelbyville, Kentucky. Take I-64 East from Louisville 31 miles. Exit 32 A to KY 55 N. Continue on KY 55 Business/ US 60 E for four miles. Right on Mack Waters Road. Left on Kentucky Street. Park is on the right.

http://www.shelbycountyparks.com/Red-Orchard-Park.html

"We continued up to a gazebo and the Spiders playground."

A colleague and good friend of mine, Carol Kaufmann, president of the Louisville Audubon Society board of directors, had alerted me to this park, which was a bit further out than most of our other excursions. Carol knew this park was a bird watcher's mecca, and had thought that we might like to explore the walking opportunities. Of course, we certainly were interested in planning a visit and eagerly looked forward to learning more about a park we had not previously been aware of.

We headed toward Shelby County on a late winter Sunday afternoon. The weather was perfect for an outdoor excursion: sunny, with just a bit of chill left in the air. We were just happy to be getting outdoors for a walk after a very long and cold winter.

We entered the park and drove past the Miller Education Center and straight down the gravel drive to park at the bottom of the hill in a parking area in front of the dog park. However, after driving around to get the lay of the land, we would recommend parking at the top of the park near the education center. By parking at the dog park, we ended up exploring the park in a bit of a disjointed manner. The trail that circles the park starts at the top of the park behind the barn and playground near the education center at the entrance. Again, we recommend following the trail in the manner in which it was meant to be walked. However, we like to just get out and start exploring, and this day was no different. So, we will walk you through the park in our somewhat disjointed way, then you can decide on your visit which areas you want to explore or if you want to walk the entire park path, which will provide a 2.5-mile walking excursion (just read through this write-up prior to your walk).

As we parked at the bottom of the hill near the dog run, that is where we picked up the mown-grass trail after spotting some other visitors heading down the path. We walked west toward a playground. Watch for mole tunnels and holes in the spongy ground (after rains, the mown grass path could be muddy so you may want to wear some sturdy waterproof boots if this is the case).

We discovered as we walked that the path connects several nature-fitness play areas. Our 11-year-old loved these playgrounds, and what was additionally unique about them was the adult-oriented exercise at each play station. Instead of parking yourself on a bench while the kiddos play, adults in groups with children can just jump on one of the elliptical machines or exercise bikes, and continue to burn some calories and keep that heart rate up.

The first play station we came upon was "Pond Life." This playground overlooks a pond and contains an informational sign with fun facts about dragonflies, turtles, and frogs. The playground itself houses a unique dragonfly seesaw and frog climbing structure. For adults, there is an air walker and power rower.

Continuing on down the path, we found a walnut grove and a bench overlooking the creek. Instead of fording the creek (as the path led down and across the creek), we backtracked past the dog run and continued up the path to a gazebo and another nature-fitness area. This one is 'Spider Playground.' It includes a webbed climbing structure. At the gazebo is an interesting "birds of prey" sign describing the wildlife habits of owls and hawks.

From there, we hiked down to Clear Creek toward the canoe launch, walking around the natural grass area, where a sign informed us that the area is a joint project of the Quail Forever and Kentucky Fish and Wildlife organizations.

I could hear the stream gurgling below, and as nothing attracts me more than rushing water, hurried to get a better view. We took a short side trail to get closer to the lively creek, the sound of water always a magnet for us.

After visiting the creek, we headed back up the hill on the grassy path, enjoying the expansive meadow views, a stiff breeze at our backs, rustling the brittle leftover leaves clinging to their tree branches.

We huffed a bit on our way up but thoroughly enjoyed the exercise and just being outdoors on this late winter afternoon with just a hint of spring in the air. We loved that birds were out in force that day, chirping happily in the distance, a sure sign of life coming back to life slowly, after enduring a very harsh winter.

As we continued back up the hill, we said hello to an elderly man with a walking cane, clipping along at a good pace—nice to see on this somewhat challenging walk.

We walked on past the dog park where our car was parked and decided to walk up to the barn and interpretive center. The large playground drew in our 11-year-old for a few minutes of play. We noticed the walking path running behind the playground and wound our way down the path.

We discovered several more nature playgrounds along the trail which delighted our entire party. Don't miss the Ant playground, with an anthill for climbing, the Bee playground, with a honeycomb climbing structure, the Caterpillar playground, with its "metamorphosis" tunnel, and our daughter's favorite, the Tree playground, with a rotted tree trunk tunnel, mushroom fairy ring and tall pine trees to climb. Each playground also contained adult exercise equipment (no resting, grownups!).

Even though we found no clear trail guidelines, we enjoyed meandering around this nature preserve, discovering all its delights in a bit of a disjointed manner. On a return visit, we stuck to the Nature Play Fitness Trail, which began behind the barn at the park's entrance. Walking the entire trail will net you about a 2.5-mile walk on a grassy path. You'll get beautiful open views, a gurgling creek, orchards, and delightful nature-themed play areas for kids and adults alike.

We were ready for a treat on the way home and, to the delight of our youngster, found a Sweet Avisha Frozen Yogurt on the way back to I-64. We might have tried going the opposite way into the quaint town of Shelbyville if we had finished up our day sooner, but were afraid that the shops would be closed on a late Sunday afternoon. The froyo hit the spot, however. We found it toward the back of a shopping strip next to Walmart on Highway 55, right before getting back on I-64 to Louisville. Note: there is also an Ice Cream and Pie Kitchen on the left side of US 60 before turning onto Highway 55—for those of you desiring a heavier treat.

This excursion was the perfect antidote to a long, enduring chill of a winter and we felt amazing after our challenging walk, and very happy to be outdoors in the sunshine once again.

RICHARD L. VISSING PARK

CLARK COUNTY, INDIANA

Walking Path: 1.5 miles, paved and gravel.

Features: Woodlands and wetlands.

Facilities: Restroom buildings at picnic pavilion. Seasonal only.

Getting there: From Louisville take I-65 North across the Kennedy Bridge to Exit 1/Jeffersonville. Stay straight on US31 N/Pearl Street. Take the ramp toward Jeffersonville/ Charlestown. Right on West 10th Street/Old IN 62. Drive 4.2 miles and turn right on Vissing Park Road. Park is ahead on right.

http://www.jeffparks.org

In the fall of 2012, work began on the newly renovated Richard L. Vissing Park. It is named for Jeffersonville's first full-time mayor, Richard Vissing, who served from 1964-1983. The park includes dense, forested woodlands in the heart of a city. There are also sports fields, a dog park, wetland areas, paved and gravel trails, two restroom buildings, open grassy areas, playgrounds, and picnic areas. Of course, the reason for our visit was to explore the nearly two miles of walking paths that wind through the park and woodlands.

The first impression I had coming into this park on an early December afternoon was surprise that this impressive recently renovated park existed tucked in an out-of-the-way area of Jeffersonville, just across the river from Louisville. A plaque at the pavilion commemorates the rededication of the park in 2013: "For our citizens to connect with nature within the heart of the city." What could be

"A plaque at the pavilion commemorates the rededication in 2013: 'For our citizens to connect with nature within the heart of the city.' What could be more perfect?"

more perfect?

Our visit was planned for a cool, but not too cold, late fall afternoon—perfect for a crisp walk after a long, lazy Thanksgiving weekend.

We parked in the main parking area in front of the picnic shelter and playground. Restroom buildings are available in this area, but were closed for the season on the day of our visit. We set out on the accessible path between the Vissing Shelter Pavilion and the landscaped retention pond. We skirted right to a blacktop walking path and around the basketball courts. The path is nicely landscaped, offering a buffer between the park and neighboring homes. It is also well-lit, with benches strategically located to allow for either a nature or sports view. Pets are allowed on a leash, and there are pet litter bags available at stations along the path.

Shortly into the path, a log bridge takes you over a wetland conservation area. We continued around the softball fields, anxious to reach the natural woodland areas at the back of the park. A gravel walk veers off at the paved trail into the woods. We took this direction, not knowing exactly where we would be heading as there are no trail direction signs. Note: There were also no trail guide brochures or maps available at the start of the path. Note to Jeffersonville Boy Scouts: we think that producing a map and/or trail signage at the park would make for a great Eagle Scout project. We were really just assuming we would not get lost in the woodlands and headed off blindly into the woods with our usual enthusiasm for a nature experience. One sign we came across did warn that no three- or four-wheeled vehicles are allowed on the trails.

At a fork in the gravel path, we continued straight on the gently winding path. Our direction offered a few gentle rises, but it was mainly a level, hard gravel path that would accommodate strollers but perhaps not wheelchairs.

We were surprised along the trail by a large-wing-spanned bird that dropped down out of the trees and glided along the path in front of us. We felt it was probably a turkey vulture—certainly an impressive creature—and very appropriate for a Thanksgiving weekend. As we continued on the path, I could hear a cacophony of birdsong in the distance and was eager to continue along into the woods.

The park's trails were fairly quiet on this Sunday afternoon, but we did run into a family out for some exercise and another gentleman out with his dog for a hike. We felt that this park might get quite busy on summer evenings with ball games in progress, but today, we thoroughly enjoyed the quiet and crisp trail walk.

There are several exit points out of the gravel woodland paths back to the developed park areas, but we continued along through the woods. I enjoyed the hypnotic sound of my own feet crunching along the gravel path. My noisiness scared several woodland creatures who scurried away hurriedly in the dry brush as I approached. The woods are dense and the trees very tall. Today, the winter sky above was blue and white, with wispy winter-cotton clouds drifting by only interrupted by the spindly paintbrush branches spreading out at the treetops.

Around the park, as we continued following the path at the back edge of the woods, we came upon the Espy Family Cemetery. It sits bizarrely in between two neighborhood homes. We could not resist investigating, so we hiked up to the wall for a closer look. Six to twelve members of the Espy family are buried here. Who were they? A sign explains that they farmed this land in the early 1800s. Interesting indeed to see this incongruous cemetery not only off the park's path, but situated as it was in between two suburban homes.

The woodland trail continues on, skirting the edge of the woods with offshoots back toward the developed park. We came suddenly upon a flock of birds roosting in the dense shrubs and could hear a woodpecker busily working away in a high tree. Much birdsong continued to serenade us as we made our way to the end of the nature trail. After approximately a mile of walking, the trail crosses a small creek—we were delighted to watch two small robins fluttering around in a small pool of water within the creek.

We walked along the edge of a large open field before turning back to the west and ending our woodland walk. The trail ends on the opposite side of the park from where you began your walk. You will see the parking area as you exit the trail.

There were numerous cut-throughs in the woods and no trail signs, but you can easily backtrack and continue a longer walk. All the paths lead back into the main developed areas of the park, so you can't get lost. We certainly enjoyed this pleasant woodland walk with some wildlife sightings.

As we made our way back to the parking area, we saw a small sign for a conservation area. This area goes through the middle of the park and through some wetlands. We couldn't resist continuing our walk to stretch our legs just a bit further. Cattails and prairie grasses grace the edge of the walkway. Knowing that this was the end of a long, relaxing four-day break from our busy, workaday world, this nature walk experience would have to last a whole week. I didn't want my time outdoors—in the chilly air, with the winter sun warm on my face as it set in the west—to end. I took several deep breaths of fresh, clean, frosty air, already looking forward to next weekend's excursion.

If you are visiting this park on a warm day, you will no doubt appreciate an ice cream treat when you are finished. There are several possibilities nearby. The closest will be Swirlz Frozen Yogurt at 2784 Meijer Drive. Drive back to 10th Street and look for the Meijer on the left. You'll find Swirlz in the shopping area near Meijer's off 10th Street. Or drive up to the light at Allison Lane and turn left to find Chillers on the left. If hot coffee or latte is more for you, head to the McDonald's on the corner at Allison Lane.

RIVERVIEW PARK

JEFFERSON COUNTY, KENTUCKY

Walking Path: Paved, 1+ miles along the
Levee Trail/Louisville Loop.

Features: Paved walking path along the Ohio River,
unique playground and picnic area overlooking a scenic area
of the Ohio River.

Facilities: Restroom building at picnic area; open seasonally only.

Getting there: Located at 8202 Greenwood Road off Cane Run
Road in southwestern Jefferson County. From downtown Louisville,
take I-64 W to Exit 1: I-264 E/Shively. Take Exit 5B/Cane Run
Road. Right on Greenwood Rd.

http://www.louisvilleky.gov/MetroParks/parks/riverview/

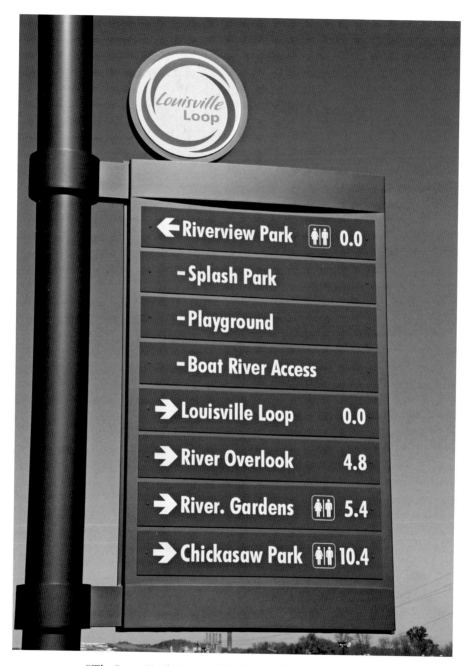

"The Levee Trail is part of the Louisville Loop. To access it, you will walk up a good-sized hill."

Coming upon yet another little gem of a park in southwestern Jefferson County was a wonderful surprise for our family. Who knew there were so many nature gems in our metro area? We were looking forward to exploring this recently renovated park in an area of town we don't get to very often.

After we left Cane Run Road for Greenwood Road and came down a slight hill toward the park, the Ohio River came into view. On the late fall morning of our visit, there was bright autumn color highlighting the forests rising on the knobs on opposite bank of the river. Scenic high rock cliffs are visible on the opposite side as well. There was definitely a "wow" factor to the beautiful view, especially as you are not far from the congestion of the city, but will feel that you are somehow miles away in a natural area.

This park has been the beneficiary of some recent improvements, including a wonderful picnic, play and spray ground—all on the banks of the Ohio River overlooking a scenic view. There are several large bench swings overlooking the river as well. It is altogether a charming and pleasant park well worth a visit to the southwestern corner of the county.

Your walk for your visit will be along the Ohio River Levee Trail, which has an access point at the park. We were so enamored with the park's amenities and scenery, however, that we decided to explore a bit before beginning our walk.

The youngster in our group naturally wanted to play on the inviting playground which was calling her name. She enjoyed the built-in nature features such as tree-stump steps, climbing rocks and a leaf-themed climbing wall. The rocks have fossils depicted on their surfaces - a nice nature touch. Another fun play structure is a large rocking boat, one of our favorite play amenities we have seen in some of the newer playgrounds we have visited. The playground is a great place for your kids or grandkids to blow off some steam before walking.

Be sure to bring a picnic lunch to this outing—you will love the pleasant picnic grounds overlooking the beautiful scenic views of the river and the hills of the southern Indiana Knobs on the opposite side. A mid or late fall day would be perfect as a bit of color in the woodlands is very appealing. Summer would have the added benefit of the spray ground for any kids or kids-at-heart in your group.

When you have had your fill of the park and are ready to walk, you will head to the western corner of the parking area and look for the access to the Levee Trail. The Levee Trail is part of the Louisville Loop. It is elevated and runs along the Ohio River Levee. To access it at Riverview Park, you will have to walk up a fairly good-sized hill to reach the level trail along the levee. Once at the top, be sure to read the signage about the knobs on the opposite side of the river. The information describes how the knobs were formed and why they do not support agriculture. This topography has not supported the same level of human population as most of the Ohio Valley. But lucky for us, it has left a very scenic legacy—part of which is Iroquois Park, not too far away.

The walking path at the top of the levee is flat and paved. A sign will point out that if you walk west you will reach the Farnsley-Moremen Landing in 3.7 miles. We had no intention of walking that far—our average walk is about 1.5 miles on these excursions. We estimate our walking speed at about one mile in 15–20 minutes. If we are not doing a loop walk, we simply watch our time and turn back after about 15 minutes. A walk of 30 minutes for us is about two miles. You may walk faster or slower than that—simply go for as long as you are comfortable, being aware that you need to plan for the same amount of time to return. Of course, a pedometer is a great option as well—turn back after one mile for a two-mile walk. Be aware that there is no shade up on this elevated trail, so be sure to take a water bottle with you. A hat or sun visor on a sunny day would also be helpful.

After we ascended the hill and decided to walk west, we went at a slow pace, enjoying the cool breezes and the elevation overlooking the river. We observed several parents with strollers, one person in a motorized wheelchair and an older gentleman riding a bicycle. There was also a dad helping his small, bike-helmeted daughter on a training-wheeled bike. We thought this would be a terrific place to learn to ride a bike.

We enjoyed our leisurely walk on this lovely, sunny, and cool afternoon. The sky was a crystal blue with the wind rattling through autumn's dry leaves still hanging on tightly to their branches. The crisp air was a signal to us that winter was truly in the air and on the way. It gave us all the more reason to appreciate the warmth of the sun and especially our time outdoors in nature.

After getting our fill of fresh air and exercise, we looked forward, as always, to finding a place for a sweet treat. We headed back out of the park along Greenwood Road and turned left once we got to Dixie Highway. We found an Orange Leaf Frozen Yogurt at 6661 Dixie Highway, on the right hand side. Orange Leaf offers lots of flavors, including seasonal favorites like pumpkin pie and gingerbread, and even includes no-sugar and dairy-free options. You pick your flavor and can top it off with over 30 different toppings such as kid-friendly gummies and "tree-hugger" granola. Something for everyone! We truly enjoy topping off our outings with a sweet treat for the ride home and left this excursion with giant smiles on our faces.

THE PARKLANDS OF FLOYDS FORK

JEFFERSON COUNTY, KENTUCKY

Getting there: Take I-64 East to exit 19B to merge onto I-265N/Gene Snyder Freeway, Exit 27 at US 60/Shelbyville Road toward Middletown/Eastwood. Turn right at the exit. Drive 1.5 miles and enter park on the right across from Valhalla Golf Course at Beckley Creek Parkway. Watch closely for park sign (easy to miss).

www.theparklands.org

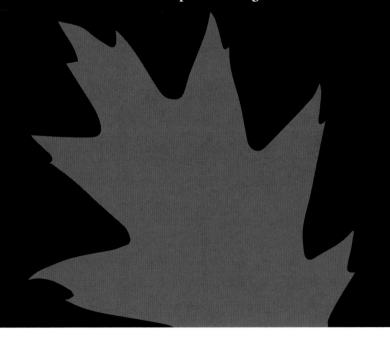

INTRODUCTION

The Parklands of Floyds Fork, located on the eastern edge of Jefferson County, opened to the public with the first of four parks in 2012. Years in the making, developed by a public-private partnership and overseen by a nonprofit group called 21st Century Parks, the Parklands, which cuts through the last major undeveloped section of metro Louisville, is a world-class addition to Louisville's parks system. Inspired by the work of Frederick Law Olmsted, the father of landscape architecture, 21st Century Parks aims to express a "contemporary and futuristic definition of beauty and function in the Floyds Fork corridor." The development, which encompasses 3,800 acres, will eventually include four major parks linked by a park drive, a first-rate urban trail system, and a unique water trail—Floyds Fork.

"Many folks shared the Loop, including walkers, joggers, bicyclers, older adults with walking canes, and a fast-moving patron on a recumbent bike."

"Be sure to note the 'Leaping Bridges'—designed to mimic the graceful leaping movements of deer."

The project is one of the largest urban park developments in the country. The master plan for the Parklands includes 100+ miles of hiking and biking trails, 19 miles of canoe trail, playgrounds, dog parks, picnic and community event facilities, accessible fishing ponds, and recreational fields. It will preserve and protect 2,000 acres of forestland, 400 acres of native meadowlands, 50 acres of wetlands, 400 acres of sustainable agriculture fields, and seven miles of stream banks. The parkway through the area is a scenic drive in itself. Be sure to note the beautiful "leaping" bridges along the way—made to mimic the graceful leaping movements of deer. The Parklands of Floyds Fork is a truly remarkable resource for the people of this region.

As of this writing, two of the parks are open to the public—Beckley Creek and Pope Lick. Beckley Creek, a wonder of walking and hiking opportunities is the park that we visited repeatedly for our walking project. Pope Lick Park contains sports and recreational fields, hiking trails, and a section of the Louisville Loop. Two additional parks, Turkey Run and Broad Run, along with a connecting natural area, the Strand, are all due to open in 2015. We can't wait!

THE LOUISVILLE LOOP IN BECKLEY CREEK

JEFFERSON COUNTY, KENTUCKY

Walking Path: Approximately 1.0 miles, paved and accessible.

Features: Scenic portion of the Loop along the Floyds Fork stream valley.

Facilities: None at trailhead; use restrooms at William F. Miles trailhead and gardens before beginning.

Getting there: Park in the North Beckley Paddling Access parking lot off the Parkway. There are signs pointing to the access, which is down a hill on the right.

This is a great walk for those who need accessibility and a smooth, paved walk. This section of the Louisville Loop fits the bill and offers a nature experience as well.

Start out at the North Beckley Paddling Access. Look for the Louisville Loop sign. If you have sure footing, take a small side trip down to the access for a good view of the stream, then backtrack to the loop. This section of the Loop meanders along Floyds Fork to the right; a steep cliff embankment is off to the left.

The day we walked this section of the Loop was a beautiful cool fall day. Many folks shared the Loop, including walkers, joggers, bicyclers, older adults with walking canes, and even one very fast-moving patron on a recumbent bike.

The stream through this portion was pretty, if a bit calmer than is my liking. I like a lively running creek, but the water was still inviting and restful as I gazed off toward the stream. There are large stone benches alongside to sit and gaze at the peaceful stream.

"This section of the Loop meanders along Floyds Fork to the right;
a steep cliff embankment is off to the left."

I noticed that there are no lights along this stretch of path; be sure to take a flashlight if walking near dusk. It will get dark quickly here with the path hidden and away from the parkway.

Continuing along the Loop will bring you first to the juncture where the Coppiced Woods trail runs into the Loop. Taking the trail will turn you back to the parking area, but involves a high woodland trail hike—not the purpose of this walk. Go a bit further until the Loop arrives at the Parkway and look to the right for a deck-like structure. Don't miss this—it's a restful overlook of a bend in Floyd's Fork. Sit a spell on the benches here and enjoy the wonderful scenic overlook before turning back and walking the way you came in. I have to admit I would have overlooked this gem if I had not been walking. Driving by this structure, it is easy to miss. There is no sign alerting passersby to stop. Sometimes you just have to get out and walk.

We really enjoyed this section of the Louisville Loop because it is so close to the waters of Floyds Fork and it is a level, accessible path. Be aware of the cyclists and joggers, however, as some are moving quite quickly and may not give much warning of their approach. We recommend hugging the edge of the path to stay out of the way of the many wheeled users of the Loop.

COPPICED WOODS TRAIL

JEFFERSON COUNTY, KENTUCKY

Walking Path: Not quite two miles, hiking trail, ups and downs, a bit more strenuous than most walks highlighted in this book.

Features: Traverses both open and dense woodlands with many "coppiced" trees (trees with more than one trunk). Trail climbs to overlook Floyds Fork and follows high cliff.

Facilities: None at trailhead; use restrooms at William F. Miles trailhead and gardens before beginning.

Getting there: Park in the small lot on the left across from the larger parking area for the North Beckley Paddling Access. You will see it shortly after entering the park from Shelbyville Road. If you park in the larger paddling access lot, you will have to climb the hill out of the parking lot to get to the start of the trail across the parkway road.

*"We learned about 'coppiced' trees. They are trees with multiple
trunks caused by nature or man."*

This is a woodland nature walk—more of a hike than a walk, but we wanted to include it for those who are interested in doing a bit more strenuous walk into nature.

At the parking area, look for the trail sign and follow the arrow to the top of the parking lot. The trail starts out as gravel but heads quickly into the woods and becomes a dirt hiking trail. We learned about the trail's namesakes, "coppiced" trees at the Creekside Center Interpretive Center. They are trees with multiple trunks, caused by nature or by man, and there are lots of them to view on this walk.

The trail winds up and down through open woods with one of the fishing lakes visible below as you enter a denser area of woods. You are walking along the park boundary, as signage points out. Watch for rocks and roots on this narrow trail. Also, it is a multiuse trail; mountain bikes are allowed. We did not see any on the day we hiked, but we noted a lot of joggers. The trail is very narrow, so watch and listen for others coming up behind you and be prepared to move quickly out of the way.

It is fairly quiet in the woods along the trail; before you know it, though, you are near the parkway road and can hear the traffic noise above. The trail is just out of view of the road. From here, you will be descending and crossing the dry stream bed several times. At about one mile, the trail goes under the parkway's bridge. Note the impressive creek rock pier supporting the bridge. It is obvious that much planning, forethought, and resources went into the esthetics of the park.

After going under the bridge, there is a sign advising that you can continue on the hiking trail which will loop back to the parking area, but it is the more difficult option. The other option is to meet up with the Louisville Loop and follow that path back to the parking area. The youngsters and photographers in our group wanted to stay with the hiking trail, so up the trail we went. It climbs a bit more steeply, with a switchback to get to the top of a ravine. All of a sudden, you will find yourself up very high, walking along a pine ridge with a rewarding view of the Floyds Fork stream valley below. The Louisville Loop path is below, along the stream. The trail goes along the cliff, so watch children carefully. We made a note to come back in the winter—this would make a nice winter walk with open views after the leaves are gone.

We left the ridge and began a descent through the woods. It was a beautiful, late October afternoon with just a slight chill in the air. The sky was a deep blue, offering a perfect background to the burnt oranges, bright yellows and reds of the fall leaves. A cool breeze rustled through the trees. I took a deep breath and stopped on the path, enjoying the moment.

Large trees stand like sentries close to the path as you wind up this nature walk. The trail ends in the Louisville Loop at the North Beckley paddling access. If you parked in the small lot above the access, you will have to walk up the roadway hill and across the parkway to your car. It is a steep climb, so be prepared. We enjoyed stretching our legs and muscles a bit more than other walks, and felt it was worth it for the scenery of the woodlands, cliff, and stream valley we traversed.

SYCAMORE TRAIL AND EGG LAWN PATH

JEFFERSON COUNTY, KENTUCKY

Walking Path: Approximately 1.5 miles. Hiking trails, mown grass paths, and paved walkways; relatively flat.

Features: Walk out on an impressive shaded gravel bar along Floyds Fork stream; Egg Lawn path goes around and through the large Egg Lawn, cut-through path explores the trees of the Egg Lawn. Soft grass offers soothing relief for tired tootsies on the way back.

Facilities: Facilities at the Creekside Center.

Getting there: Plenty of parking at the Creekside Center/ Marshall Playground across from the Egg Lawn, approximately in the middle of Beckley Creek Park.

This area is the heart of the new Beckley Creek Park. We would suggest if you have children with you that you will want to allow some time to explore the PNC Achievement Center for Education and Interpretation and the Marshall Play/ Sprayground at the Creekside Center before beginning your walk. There are picnic tables available at the playground, and a picnic lunch is a perfect way to relax and enjoy this area of the park.

The Sycamore Trail begins at the intersection of Beckley Creek Parkway and the Egg Lawn access road. The trail heads quickly back toward the stream.

We began down the hiking path on a warm, late-summer afternoon. A bright yellow butterfly danced in front of us, leading the way. We looked up to see a trio of the beauties fluttering in the shrubs, enjoying the last taste of summer warmth. The path quickly entered a welcoming and cool shaded woods. A breeze ruffled

"The girls (including Mom) kicked off their shoes and walked through the cool grass barefoot. Heavenly!"

the leaves gently. The trail was crowded with many hikers and joggers on the path. It seemed like everyone was out on this day to explore this wonderful new nature resource in our community.

This is an interesting walk. The trail takes you fairly quickly to a large gravel bar. Children and children-at-heart will love this sandy access to the stream's water. This is also a good place to look for mussel shells, some of which are quite large. We found a complete, intact double shell approximately three inches wide on the day of our visit. Walk all the way to the end of the gravel bar and you will be rewarded with a nice open view of the stream; it almost looks like a small lake here. Our younger daughter could not resist tossing in a few rocks and poking around in the water with her ever-present stick.

We spent a good amount of time on the gravel bar gazing at the swirling pools of water, finding shells, and just enjoying being up close to the water. But, a word of caution—even though this is a very easy walk, it is not paved. Be careful of roots and rocks along the trail and watch your steps carefully.

The path continues back up to the road and you may want to continue your walk by crossing over the parkway to the Egg Lawn path. We chose to do this and walked around the lawn counterclockwise to the middle of the lawn where there is a cut through a small woodland area. We thoroughly enjoyed the beautiful open views around the Egg Lawn, and especially the fall colors of reds, golds and, yellows in the planted and native trees.

We had been on several walks on this warm afternoon, and our feet were getting hot in our hiking shoes. The lawn looked so cool and inviting that the girls (including Mom) kicked off their shoes and walked through the cool grass barefoot. Heavenly! The grass in the lawn was nearly as soft as moss. It cooled and tickled our toes and we giggled all the way across the lawn. Looking around the lawn at the expansive views on our way back to where we had parked our car near the playground, I thought to myself that if there is one word to describe the effort to create this incredible new park, that word is BRAVO!

HUMANA GRAND ALLEE COUNTRY LANE WALK

JEFFERSON COUNTY, KENTUCKY

Walking Path: Approximately one-mile loop,
mostly paved, relatively flat.

Features: Walk along Country Lane, over an impressive wetland
boardwalk, and through wildflower meadows.

Facilities: Portable toilet at farthest parking area near the
junction of the Promenade and Louisville Loop. We would
recommend using the facilities at the Creekside Center
before starting this walk.

Getting there: From Shelbyville Road entrance,
continue toward the Egg Lawn and turn left before the
Creekside Center. Cross the "leaping" bridge. Look for signs to
Humana Grand Allee. There are two parking areas to the right
along the Grand Allee. Park in the first one if there is a space—
this lot is smaller than the farther lot, but is closer to the
Humana Legacy Commons, where we began this walk.

We arrived to explore this area on a picture-perfect late fall afternoon. We had no idea what to expect on this more formal "Grand Allee" walk. And just what, you may ask—as we did—is a Grand Allee? Well, from the best French translation we could find, a large path. And that it is. But the term adds some ambiance as it also implies a stateliness to the venue, designed to be the "best walk in Louisville." This path is part of the Country Lane that runs through this area of the park. A visit to the Humana Legacy Commons area highlights the ambience with a large, circular decorative fountain engraved with park donor names and surrounded by built-in benches.

The Country Lane walk is to the east of the fountain. The path is called The Festival Promenade and is a wide gravel lane bordered by landscaping, benches, and tall streetlights. Strolling is the order of the day for this walk. You will come to a

"It felt almost like an ocean boardwalk because of the openness
and breezes over the water."

long, graceful boardwalk over an open expanse of pond wetlands. Cattails and lily pads grace the edges, and fish are clearly visible below in the water. It felt almost like an ocean boardwalk because of the openness and breezes over the water. You won't find a nature walking experience quite like this anywhere in the Louisville area, and we really enjoyed it.

There are several side trails to the north and south of the main boardwalk path. We meandered down several (and were told later by a helpful guide in the Creekside Center that there are hundreds of these small side trails to enjoy throughout the park). There were smaller boardwalks across shallower parts of the wetlands and through wildflower meadows on these side trails. On this warm afternoon, we were graced with fields of still-blooming bright yellow black-eyed Susans. Thousands of grasshoppers were also out in abundance, while bees and butterflies flitted here and there looking for that last, late-summer drop of nectar wherever they could find it. Did they know that exactly one week later, the temperature would drop below freezing and our area would be hit with an early-fall winter blast and hard freeze? Perhaps the insects do know these things; they certainly seemed to be very busy on this warm day.

The sun was very bright this afternoon, but the breezes cool; fall was waning and it made me a bit sad. The bright colorful leaves would soon be leaving us as winter approached. Our feet crunched pleasantly along the gravel path as I took a deep breath of fresh air and continued this very enjoyable walk. Ahead of us came the happy sound of laughter wafting across the field from our two young girls skipping ahead with a rambunctious new puppy. I felt gratified that the older of the two girls—a twenty-year-old—had been through her "not-doing-anything-with-the-folks stage, and was here today, enjoying nature and spending time with her middle-aged parents and a younger sister. Maybe this mom did a few things right after all, I thought.

At the end of the promenade, there are a few picnic tables which make a good spot to stop and enjoy a snack or lunch before continuing this walk along the

Louisville Loop. You will follow the sidewalk and then turn right onto the Loop to continue. A sign informed us that, at this point, we were at Mile Number 71.2 on the Louisville Loop. The Loop will eventually be 100 miles and encircle Louisville.

Once on the Loop, be aware that you will now be sharing your path with cyclists, and there are a lot of them. Stay on the sides of the sidewalk to avoid any collisions. Several times on this day, we heard brakes screeching when cyclists had to make sudden stops. If you want to avoid this, simply turn around at the picnic tables and walk back the way you came, staying on the Country Lane. We soldiered on because we are always interested in walking new paths and we enjoy the sense of discovery. We were not to be disappointed today, either.

As you walk along the Loop, your reward on this portion of the walk is a marvelous, expansive view across meadows and of the gracefully curving path that unfolds in front of you. I was amazed at how restful this open view was to my eyes. Your vision is allowed to roam across the fields with nothing blocking your view until your eyes reach the far woodlands. The path offers an offshoot down to a view of Floyds Fork, which runs along the loop at this section.

Small white meadow daisies bent forward gracefully to kiss us as we passed by. An intriguing sign pointed us in the direction of the "Sassafras Bosque." We decided to take this side path to investigate. Another word we were unfamiliar with: *bosque.* Looking it up later, we learned that it means "formally planted grove of trees in gardening." Makes sense. And that is just what we found—a fragrant stand of sassafras trees. Our girls delighted in the fragrance of root beer emanating from a few crushed leaves and twigs fallen on the ground. Delightful! Children will love this sensory experience. And we would have completely missed it if we had not been willing to explore just a little off the beaten path.

We meandered around the path, serenaded by the rhythmic and surprising clicks of thousands of seed pods popping open in the field on this late fall day. It was so surprising we had to stop and listen, marveling at this unusual phenomenon. It was something we had never experienced before—another nature experience we certainly could not have without our walking shoes carrying us down a meandering path. I was delighted with this walk in so many ways, but then I am rarely disappointed in any nature walk. I sometimes wish I could just live outdoors.

After crossing a small creek, we returned to the Promenade Path. Your adventure on this walk may or may not take exactly the same path as ours, but it will be enjoyable no matter which way you wander, and you will not get lost. I mentally added up all the unique features of this deceptively simple walk which included so many sights (expansive views), sounds (popping seed pods, jumping insects), and smells (fragrant sassafras). This was truly one for the senses! The only thing missing was taste, and you know we had that covered with our reward for walking—ice cream! More about that at the end of this section on the Parklands.

VALLEY OF THE GIANTS TRAIL

JEFFERSON COUNTY, KENTUCKY

Walking Path: Approximately 1.5 miles, compacted dirt and paved, relatively flat.

Features: Walk through woodland area of old-growth giant sycamore trees, along Floyds Fork, and through an agricultural meadow.

Facilities: No restrooms at trailhead. Use facilities at the Creekside Center located near the Egg Lawn.

Getting there: To get to the trailhead, take the park road past the fishing lakes, under I-64 and skirt the Egg Lawn to the left. Continue left over the "leaping" bridge and past the Humana Grand Allee to the southernmost parking area. If you pass Trestle Point, you've gone too far.

Alternatively, you may also enter the park from Taylorsville Road and Pope Lick Road or South English Station at the southern end. Coming in from this direction, you will find the trail kiosk and parking area near the gate on the right.

"This is a stream valley filled with giants who have been standing along this creek for eons. What a fantastic sight."

The Valley of the Giants Trail is just a little over six-tenths of a mile long and rated easy. The walk can be extended through an agricultural field and return along the Louisville Loop, making your walk about 1.5 miles long.

The trail begins near the Sara and W. L. Lyons Brown Bridge near the south end of Beckley Creek Park. There is a parking lot near the trailhead but no facilities at this location. In fact, we did not find any facilities on the southern end of the park. You will have to head back to the Creekside Center for restrooms, so be sure to take care of that before starting out on this walk.

You will start out on this walk by walking around an agricultural field to get to the start of the hiking trail. Simply follow the path and the signs toward the Valley of the Giants trail. On the early fall morning of our visit, the breeze was cool and trees were starting to turn. The field we walked around to get to the trail was filled with golden soybeans. Reflected in the autumn sun, it was a beautiful burnished gold. The Sting song, "Fields of Gold" was running through my head as I started off down the meadow path. It was fun to get up close and personal with the yellow-gold soybean plants. After walking a short way along the field, we arrived at the start of the Valley of the Giants Trail. I was anxious to see these "giants" for myself.

The path starts out wide and is relatively smooth, walking along a compacted dirt trail, but watch your footing along the natural dips in the earth. A family with a stroller in tow moved right along with no problem, but we would not recommend trying to take a wheelchair on this path.

Immediately to the left of the trail is a side path to a log structure. It is interesting, but we could not determine what its purpose was. Back on the main path, we let several groups of hikers pass us by. It was a popular trail this morning. Coming into view quickly was Floyds Fork—the water streaming by was a welcome sight. A cacophony of raucous birdsong serenaded us as we walked along the winding path. Trees with twisted, exposed roots leaned over the creek at odd angles along the bank. Vines dripped from canopies above our heads and hung from twisted branches, giving this walk a somewhat eerie and gothic feel, even with the sun streaming through the high branches.

We came to several of the trail's namesake "giants." Huge trees along this path don't disappoint. Trunks are massively wide, and the trees soar skyward. And there are lots of them. It is no lie: this is a stream valley filled with giants who have been standing along this creek for eons. What a fantastic sight. Who knew we had these massive trees growing in our backyard? We were amazed to think these monsters had been here for at least our entire lifetimes and probably for generations before us, and that there probably had been no access to view these wonderful creations of nature until the developed Parklands came along.

It is obvious that this valley has seen much flooding; some of the tree trunks are literally twisted and oddly formed, many have split trunks, some with grotesque bulbous growths. We thought it would be fantastic to walk along this trail on a gloomy late November afternoon when the light was waning.

But on this day, the sun was shining and leaves were falling gracefully, one, two at a time, twisting lightly on their way down. Our 11-year-old played a family favorite: "Catch the Falling Leaves." Every fall, when the leaves fall, we have played this game. All we do is simply try to catch the leaves as they fall to the ground. It is surprisingly hard to do—they trick you. You will think that a leaf is going to land right in your hand, and then it just lifts back up into the air, teasing you as if to say, "Ha ha, you can't catch me."

Watch your footing for giant hedge apples fallen in the path, and be aware that this is also a multiuse trail allowing for trail bikes to come through. Several did on our walk; luckily, the riders called out ahead so that we could quickly move to the side to let them through.

We enjoyed this walk not only for the "giants," but also because it skirts along the creek—and we love a creek walk. At about .5 miles, there is a small rapids in the stream. We can't resist the sound of rushing water and loved that we could get close to it here. As we neared the end of the valley trail, we took note of the unusual features of this excursion: a wide stream on one side, a field of gold on the other, while walking through a woodland valley of gigantic trees.

The trail ends by opening up into the middle of the agricultural field. At this point, you may either backtrack through the valley along the hiking trail to head back to your car, or you may continue on a narrow path through the middle of the field and circle back to your car along the sidewalk, which is also part of the Louisville Loop. We could not resist an opportunity to meander across the field of gold again, so we chose the long way back and enjoyed some lovely open vistas. If you do choose to go back this way, be aware that there is no shade for about .6 mile. You will be walking in the open meadow and then along the roadway where there are no shade trees.

We enjoyed this way as a different view from the woodland trail, but were grateful for having thrown some sunglasses in our fanny pack before departing. We enjoyed a bit longer walk as well. For us, 1.5 miles feels just about right for a nature walk. It was back to our car to eagerly plan what to explore next in this amazing park.

Time for Ice Cream!

After walking the paths of Beckley Woods in the Parklands, especially on a warm, sunny day, you will probably be ready for a yummy ice cream treat. We suggest you head back to Shelbyville Road and turn left toward Middletown. There is a Graeter's Ice Cream (one of our favorites) at 13817 English Villa Drive. It's on the left after passing S. English Station Road.

Graeter's offers rich, small-batch ice cream with lots of all-natural ingredients. Decadent flavors such as Original Salted Caramel, Elena's Blueberry Pie, and Madagascar Bourbon Vanilla Bean are favorites. Some locations are now offering new low-glycemic, 50%-less-sugar flavors—ask about them. We recommend spending a bit more time with your family (or walking friends) with a cool sweet treat in hand before heading back to your "real" world. We know a return visit to the beautiful Parklands won't be long in your future.

SAUNDERS SPRINGS NATURE PRESERVE

HARDIN COUNTY, KENTUCKY

Walking Path: About two miles, gravel and hiking trails.

Features: Spring-fed water cascades, lake and pond, rustic trails, scenic terrain, native plants, and woodlands.

Facilities: Restrooms available at upper and lower parking areas.

Getting there: 100 Saunders Springs Lane off North Wilson Road in Radcliff, Kentucky 41 miles south of Louisville. Park is located between 31W (Dixie Highway) and Fort Knox.

http://www.kentuckytourism.com/do/saunders-springs-nature-preserve/10805/

We stumbled upon a brochure for this off-the-beaten-path nature preserve one afternoon while enjoying a treat at the Star Café in West Point, Kentucky. The brochure was intriguing. A nature preserve in our area with spring-fed cascading streams, dramatic terrain, 11 trails, picnic pavilions, and fishing ponds that we weren't aware of? Well, naturally, we had to find out more and decided to make a visit as soon as possible. We were not disappointed when we headed to Radcliff several weeks later and discovered a wonderful natural resource.

Saunders Springs Nature Preserve is owned by the city of Radcliff, Kentucky, and is managed by the Radcliff Forestry and Conservation Board. It is a 26-acre preserve completely surrounded by the Fort Knox Military Reservation. The property is the site of an old water plant for the city, which went out of commission in 1968. It was deeded to the city of Radcliff in 1992 and opened to the public as a nature preserve in 2002.

The preserve is open year-round with no admission fee. You will be delighted with the scenic viewing and walking opportunities here. There is a spectacularly diverse terrain, including a deep canyon, woodlands with native ferns, an upper lake, and a lower pond. There are rock outcrops and 11 mostly short (one-third mile or so) hiking trails for all levels of ability. The preserve also offers picnic pavilions, restroom buildings, several 1880s-era log cabins, fishing, scout camping, and a Kentucky native plants garden. A welcome center is currently under development.

We arrived for our visit on a picture-perfect mid-October afternoon with a bright blue sky, sunshine, color in the trees, and cool temperatures. Our youngster had decided to sit this walk out, opting instead to stay home with her older sister, who had brought over her new puppy. The girls wanted puppy playtime, so the two middle-age parents went out for the afternoon without their ever-present young hiking buddy. Get used to it, I told myself. This is the way it's going to be soon— just us two old folks out for a Sunday afternoon drive and walk in the woods. Well, that doesn't sound so bad, I added to myself. I am so very thankful for my love of nature and the physical ability to get out and enjoy it.

"We found surprises along every small path."

Upon entering the preserve, we passed the three 1880s-era log cabins, opting to save the exploration of these historic structures for after our walk. We continued on the park drive, which is narrow and twisting but offers good scenic views over some spectacular terrain, including a canyon. The road has some steep declines toward the back of the preserve and finally ends at the lower level, where you will find a picnic pavilion, restroom building, and the old water plant, which looks like a squat water tower sitting on the ground.

We got out and explored a bit of the scenery around the parking area. We marveled at the very pretty cascading streams and small waterfalls just a few steps from our car.

I wandered over to the Kentucky native plants garden located just off the parking area, to observe the last remaining blooms hanging on to the season for a little while longer. I noted such plantings as goldenrod, Indian hemp, iris, snowberry, aster, rue, larkspur, foam flower, blazing star, and a large Kentucky coffee tree. If you are visiting in season, don't miss this.

There are numerous options for walking from this area. Several trails start and end near the parking area. Most offer walks of three-tenths of a mile to a half mile, but you can certainly combine several trails for a longer walk. We wanted to explore as many as possible, and we were not disappointed in any of them.

The Tranquility Trail is a short, accessible trail that begins behind the restroom building and merges into the Fern Trail. This path follows along a pretty cascade, which on this day was roaring after a week of heavy rain. It was truly lovely. As we walked along the trail, we noticed a cave in the cliff along the stream. Be sure to look over to the right of the trail so you don't miss this. The trail continues around the holding pond near the old water plant building. Along the tall wooded embankments, you can observe at least seven varieties of native ferns. It is an impressive hillside. The trail eventually loops back to the parking area and, once again, we had to decide which path to take.

We wandered across the roadway to a rustic bridge overlooking another beautiful cascade, which was crowned above by yet another bridge—a very pretty scene and a good place for a photo opportunity. In fact, there was a photographer at the site taking photos of a family group while we were there. The backdrop in their photos was surely delightfully scenic.

We saw a trail sign for the Cascade Trail ahead and decided to give it a try. The sign alerted us that there were 60 steps up on this trail. Since we had just returned from a week of hiking in the Great Smoky Mountains National Park, we thought this would be no problem for master hikers such as ourselves. At least that's what we told ourselves as we huffed and puffed up those steps. We made it up to the top and were rewarded with beautiful views upstream and downstream. You will want to take your time getting up the steps to catch your breath.

At the top, you will see a pretty scene: the larger lake, used to be a reservoir for the water plant, is straight ahead. A gravel walking path continues around the lake. I walked slowly this day, savoring the dappled sunlight through the woods and letting my eyes alight on the last bits of wildflower color along the forest floor. A fisherman ahead of me pulled a good-size fish out of the water. Nice one, I told him. It was a bluegill, he told me, and "an eater." But then he threw it back in the water.

I realized I had somehow become separated from my photographer husband, which is not unusual for us on our walks. I enjoy my solitude in nature, and today was no different. I sat for a while on a well-placed bench along the trail, enjoying the lake view and gentle breezes.

Continuing on, I came across a rustic bridge. Stopping in the middle and looking out toward the lake, I was rewarded with a wonderful view of a line of turtles out sunning themselves on a log.

The trail continues around the lake but branches off in different directions, and you will have to decide which of these to explore. Trail signs along the way provide great descriptions, however, so choosing won't be hard. The signs also tell you how many steps are involved each direction. We found surprises along every small path, including bridges, boardwalks over wetlands, climbs with well-made steps up to great views, and even a rock outcrop over the lake. That one was my favorite, and it was a bit hidden, so I was delighted to come across it unexpectedly. The flat rock juts out into the lake, offering a nice spot to stop and soak up nature for a few minutes. I took the opportunity to be still and let the beauty of the day permeate my soul: the water rippled ever so gently from a soft breeze across the lake. The early fall hues in the treetops were reflected in the lake, a few crickets chirped, acorns dropped into the water, a turtle gurgled as it dove off its sunny spot on the log into the cool water of the sun-dappled lake: it was an explosion of nature to delight my senses. I wished I could just bottle it up and keep it forever.

I meandered up a steep embankment—up 120 steps, according to the trail sign—and was rewarded with a view of an impressive old-growth "stave oak" (more commonly known as a white oak), a huge and towering oak tree keeping watch over the lake below. A sign at the base of the tree informs hikers that it is three to four feet in trunk diameter and soars 80–100 feet up in the air.

I descended back to the lake and rejoined my walking partner, and we continued around the lake and ended up at the Tranquility Trail, which we had already walked earlier in the day. We were near our car in the parking area. We caught our breath for a few moments and reflected on the beauty of this small nature preserve.

The people of Radcliff have a special place in this rugged bit of preserved nature, and it is obvious that they appreciate and care for it. The park has many well-maintained amenities. Signage is some of the most informative we have ever seen in a park. The nature preserve is rustic and scenic and feels like a fairy forest with its lovely bridges, boardwalks, benches, ferns, streams, and cascades. We were delighted to have discovered this lovely day-hiking spot.

We drove out of the lower part of the park back to the entrance and got out of our car to explore the log cabins, which are well-preserved and rustic. We had spent considerably more time at this rustic preserve than we had planned but were very glad we had made the trip and vowed to come back. Next time we knew our little hiking buddy would not want to miss it.

On your way out, you will find a few choices for an ice cream treat. There is a Baskin- Robbins on Gold Vault Road in Fort Knox. There is also a Starbucks in Fort Knox. We opted for snack blizzards at Dairy Queen at the intersection of Highways 1638 and 31W (Dixie Highway) on our way back to Indiana via Mauckport.

WAVERLY PARK

JEFFERSON COUNTY, KENTUCKY

Walking Path: Approximately half a mile, compacted gravel, completely accessible.

Features: Woodlands, bridges, lake, and fishing shelter. Facilities: Portable only.

Getting there: Dixie Highway to Third Street Road. Turn east on Arnoldtown Road. Park is on the left.

http://www.louisvilleky.gov/MetroParks/parks/waverly/

We call this walk our Waverly Park *redo* because we covered this park in our first book, *Take A Hike, Louisville!* At that time, the Metro Louisville Parks Department had just completed Phase I of a $500,000 renovation around the lake area, and we wanted to see how the landscaping had fared. We were anxious to see the fruits of the labor that had built a walking trail around the lake, an accessible fishing pier and grassy picnic areas around the lake banks.

Waverly Park is not part of the Waverly Hills Sanatorium property, although the two properties butt up against each other in some areas. Nothing spooky or ghostly about this little-known gem in the southwestern part of Jefferson County. The park is managed as part of the Jefferson Memorial Forest, and we could see why. The park includes a large, rugged, hilly and densely forested section offering some amazing mountain bike trails. If mountain biking is your thing, this is the

"Our daughter no longer pretended to be the forest fairy; instead she was Katniss Everdeen, of The Hunger Games."

park for you. We enjoyed simply driving along the twisting park road through the forest to arrive at the lake and picnic area at the back of the park, for our late summer afternoon walk. The drive is about two miles to this developed area, which includes the lake, picnic pavilion, playground, and fishing pier. There is a parking area on the right, across from the picnic pavilion.

We parked and began our outing on a warm, dry, and windy afternoon with a loud chirring cicada cacophony serenading us as we set out. The lake was sparkling in the distance and a winding path beckoned in front of us. A stiff breeze ruffled the leaves on branches overhead as we started down the path. We knew a weather front was moving in, about to end our spell of hot and sticky temperatures. The first taste of cooler fall breezes was on the way.

We gazed out on the lake as we approached, noticing three long-necked geese lazing languidly, seeming to simply drift along on the surface. We turned left and started around the lake after crossing a small overflow creek. Several frogs popped their heads up out of the water as we walked by. Our 11-year-old looked around for a stick. She is not too old to poke around in the water.

Continuing on, you will come to a wooden bridge. On this day, the bridge was bordered by late-summer jewelweed, with its telltale bright orange berries. Large, fluffy cattails pushed up between the orange clumps.

Across the bridge is a small frog pond where you may observe large purple pond plantings with flat green leaves (almost like a lily pad) and dramatic purple flower spikes pushing skyward. After a bit of research, we identified it as purple pickerelweed. Very pretty!

The path continues on into the woodlands behind the lake. Our daughter noticed a huge tree on the banks with elephantine roots, which she said looked like legs. The trees on this side of the lake, as part of the forested area, are old-growth trees with huge trunks. They soar to the sky. We enjoyed standing at their bases and gazing up to the heavens.

The lake sparkled through the trees on this sunny and breezy afternoon. The parks department has built lovely fishing alcoves along the banks with large stone benches, which are always full of folks either fishing, picnicking, or just enjoying the lake.

The walking path continues in a gentle curving up-and-down rise. A skink with a bright teal streak crossed our trail and vanished into the forest flora. We noticed a few red-gold leaves fallen on the path—another sure sign of the change of seasons shortly upon us.

The leaves rustled stiffly with the breeze as we passed a mountain biking offshoot trail into the woods. We enjoyed the peacefulness of this walk, with the forest providing shade and rustling leaves on one side and the lake's gentle lapping on the other, a nature melody to go along with the rhythm of our walking steps. I walked leisurely and breathed in the forest before returning to the more open side of the lake.

The geese on the lake honked loudly from across the other side of the lake, and children's laughter drifted across from the play area. A dog was let off his leash to make a mad dash into the lake for a cooling swim on this very warm day.

Our daughter with her stick no longer pretended to be the forest fairy that was her favorite on hikes years ago. No, now she is Katniss Everdeen of *The Hunger Games* with her bow and arrow, hiding among the trees. A new fantasy heroine for the girl, not quite on fire, but nevertheless growing up way too fast.

Crossing over a rustic iron bridge on the far side of the lake takes you over another spillway. Your walk is a short loop around the lake. If you are inclined to stay in the woodland area, simply turn around at the bridge and retrace your steps along the far side of the lake.

We chose to continue over the bridge and cross to the fishing pier on the other side of the lake. We looked over the bridge into the lake's water to view hundreds of small fish. Our feet crunched a bit too loudly as we passed a couple of fisherman talking quietly. A sign encouraged users of the park to practice "angler ethics." We reminded ourselves that we needed to tread softly as fishing is a quiet and respectful business.

A beautiful blue-and-tan dragonfly cut across our line of vision as we approached the pier. The pier and pavilion are handicap-accessible and offer a peaceful place to sit under shade and view the lake and forest.

This walk, while not long, is a worthwhile relaxing interlude in your day. We felt like it offered a forest oasis in the middle of the surrounding suburban neighborhoods. It feels like an out-of-the-way retreat and is very enjoyable.

For an ice cream treat after your walk, we recommend Valley Dairy Freeze on Deering Road, about six miles away. To get there, turn right out of the park on Arnoldtown Road. Turn right at Third Street Road. Continue onto Valley Station Road and turn left on Deering Road. The Dairy Freeze is on the right. This is a roadside soft-serve shop with a variety of shakes, malts, sundaes, flurries, cones, and other frozen novelties. Perfect after a warm afternoon walk.

WENDELL MOORE PARK

OLDHAM COUNTY, KENTUCKY

Walking Path: Two miles, paved and gravel.

Features: Large lake, woodlands, meadows, and wetland areas.

Facilities: Rustic restrooms near picnic shelter at lake. Seasonal only.

Getting there: 1551 N. Highway 393, Buckner, Kentucky (approximately 18 miles from Louisville). From Louisville take I-71 North to Exit 18/Buckner, turn left on Highway 393, then left again on Route 146 West, then right on 393 N. Park is on the right—enter at the aquatic pool center.

http://www.oldhamcountyky.gov/P&R/Parks/WM%20BH. htm

This 107-acre park in Oldham County sits on the site of the John W. Black community and aquatic centers. It is a lovely recreational park with walking paths, picnic shelters, tennis courts, sports fields, playgrounds, horseshoe pits, and a large fishing lake (Reformatory Lake) with pier. You will see the aquatic pool on your left as you enter.

Upon arriving, drive straight back and under the archway. There is a large parking area near the lake with two picnic pavilions and a playground nearby. You will want to spend some time at this very lovely picnic area overlooking Reformatory Lake. Plan to bring a picnic lunch or at least a snack to enjoy before or after your walk.

On the day of our visit, it was a chilly late winter afternoon; the aquatic center

"We always walk out on piers; they afford a good view of the water and sometimes we can see fish swimming by below."

long closed for the season. We started out walking on the connector trail along the lake. You can pick up this gravel trail at any point along the lake. Head east (right) toward the football field. You will be walking toward a new area of paved nature paths recently opened in the natural area.

Along the lake there are several piers. We always walk out on piers when we come across them; they usually afford a good view of the water and sometimes we can see fish swimming by below. This one was no different, and we enjoyed a few calming moments here.

Back on the trail, you will find it to be up and down with some ruts. Watch footing closely. The lake on your left is large and scenic, but we have to admit we found the Lagrange Reformatory across the lake sitting up on a hill to be just a bit foreboding.

As I walked along on this cold, but clear afternoon, the gravel crunching beneath my feet, I sighed deeply. I love meandering down a never-before-discovered trail. Just like going in a new direction in life, I embrace change and look forward to whatever new, undiscovered pathways and attractions might lie ahead. I felt this sense of anticipation today.

I appreciated the magic of nature in bringing a father and college-age daughter together on this day. They walked ahead of me, their heads together huddled over camera equipment, engrossed in analyzing just the right way to get the best shot— nature photography bringing them together when nothing else in life could.

Our younger daughter was perfectly content as well, walking along with her ever-present stick, poking it in every hole with even a minuscule amount of water, and scribbling in the soft sand beneath the gravel. Each of us went along slowly down the path in our own little worlds, enjoying being outdoors again on a beautiful day after enduring many long winter days.

At the end of the lake, the trail turns and continues up a hill to the start of the new paved walking paths. At the top of the hill, you will have several options consisting of loop trails of various distances, the longest of which is one mile. We chose to explore the longest.

There is a bit of hilly up and down on these paved trails; just take it slow and steady. Making it up to the top of the hill awards you with an expansive view. It is very restful for your eyes to look out over the hilly landscape with the lake sparkling in the distance. Continuing on, the path meanders alongside a woodland area and then winds around to adjacent farmland. Cows were grazing on the hill on the day we walked, and our girls went through the woods to a fence to get a closer look.

Follow your path back around to the start of the loops. With its climbs, this walk is perhaps a bit more challenging than some, but it is well worth the effort for the beautiful landscape and expansiveness of the views offered along the way. You will have stretched your legs quite a bit by the time you descend the loop trails and walk back along the lake to return to your car in the parking area.

Our girls were looking forward to their ice cream treat, but alas, we didn't find a dedicated ice cream parlor on way back to I-71. They were not too disappointed, however, when we came upon a Starbucks at Exit 14/Buckner. The girls were happy with frozen vanilla bean frappes. Mom was thrilled just to get a great cup of hot coffee for the ride back to town. All in all, this makes for a wonderful afternoon outing, especially nice on a chilly but sunny winter day.

WILLIAM H. GRAHAM PARK: LAKE LOLA WALKING PATH

SCOTT COUNTY, INDIANA

Walking Path: .75 mile, paved.

Features: Scenic lake, picnic ground, and historic rail line site.

Facilities: Restroom building at the Car House exhibit.

Getting there: I-65 N to Exit 29 (Scottsburg/Salem), approximately 30 miles north of Louisville. Right on W. McClain Avenue. Left on US Highway 31N. Third right on Lakeshore Drive. Left onto N. Hyland Street (becomes Lakeshore Drive S.). Left on Bond. Look for parking on the right.

https://www.facebook. com/.../William-H-Graham-Park.../263006540455.

This small and lovely city park is named for the well-loved mayor of Scottsburg, Indiana, William Graham, who has been mayor since 1988. The park offers a scenic lake with a paved walking path, a lovely picnic/playground area and a historical rail site. This park is a bit hard to find, as it is tucked into a neighborhood area of Scottsburg, but once you come across it, you won't be disappointed.

We arrived for our visit on a very chilly early fall Saturday morning. Only a few intrepid folks were out for a walk or jog this morning. The park was nearly deserted.

From the parking area, you will see the lake—which has a dam in the middle— on your left, picnic grounds, the walking path, and the historic rail site very near the parking area. We bundled up and got out to explore this site first, which is an old train station building, or car house, as it is called. Note: There are also restroom facilities located near the car house, which were open even on this after-season day.

"It was bitterly cold this morning, but that's the way it is with weather. We usually do not let it dictate whether we will have an outing or not."

The unusual car house is on the site of the old Lake Iola Interurban Rail, which was once a stopover along the Louisville-to-Indianapolis rail line in the early 1900s. Lake Iola was actually built to provide a water supply for power equipment. There is a restored train car in the car house, and a remnant of the rail line is still visible. An accessible ramp allows everyone to get up to the train car and take a peek inside.

After spending a little time exploring this interesting piece of history, we were on to our walk. It was bitterly cold this morning, and we were not prepared for it to be so cold this early in the fall. But that's the way it goes with weather, and we usually do not let the weather dictate (too much) whether we will have an outing or not, so on we walked.

We started out toward the picnic area. A sign along the path advised that there is no swimming, wading, or rock throwing in the lake (Darn, exclaimed our youngster—throwing rocks in water is one of her favorite nature activities). There are no bikes or skateboards allowed on the path. A small pier and gazebo allow walkers to get out over the water a bit. A pair of ducks braved the chilly water below us.

We walked along the lake to the picnic area. It is a scenic area with large trees overlooking the lake. If it had been warmer, we would have loved a picnic lunch here. We would certainly recommend bringing your lunch to enjoy in this pleasant spot if you are walking on a warm afternoon. If you have children in your group, plan to spend some time before or after walking here. The playground has some unusual play structures, one of which is a hamburger. None of our group had ever seen a climbable hamburger before! A manmade waterfall in the middle of the area is a nice touch. Today, our 11-year-old complained of being too cold to swing. Keep walking, I told her. For once, she did not complain at being shuffled away from a playground.

We continued around the path, and had to go around a group of geese snacking on dry corn someone had scattered along the path. Fitness stations are available along the lake for those inclined to add a little more physical activity to their walk.

I stopped and did a few of the recommended side bends at one post to loosen a stiff neck. Ahh, that felt good.

The dam in the middle of the lake offers a shorter walk by taking the path across it and heading back, but we chose to go around the entire lake for a bit longer walk.

Either way, this is an easy, accessible, and very pleasant walk and a nice park to visit. At the end of the loop, the path stops at the road; be sure to look for traffic before heading back around to the parking lot and your car.

On your way out of town, you may want to first visit the picturesque town of Scottsburg. It boasts a pretty square with shops and eateries. For your ice cream treat, there is a Chillers on the way out. Head back to I-65 on West McClain. Go past the intersection to I-65, and you will see it on the left (1515 W. McClain Avenue). Chillers offers sandwiches, hot dogs, premium soft-serve and seasonal hand-dipped treats.

ADDITIONAL WALKING PATHS FROM *TAKE A HIKE, LOUISVILLE!*

The following nature walks are covered in detail in our previous book, *Take A Hike, Louisville!* We include brief descriptions and updates here on these wonderful walking paths, appropriate for the older walker, as well as those with small children or differently abled folks in tow.

ANCHORAGE TRAIL

JEFFERSON COUNTY, KENTUCKY

Walking Path: Two miles, paved.

Features: Meadows, stream valley, lake, gardens

Facilities: None.

Getting there: Highway 146 (Lagrange Road) from the Lyndon area east to Anchorage. Turn left on Evergreen Avenue after the post office and park across from park area.

The Anchorage Trail was built by John Schnatter, a.k.a. Papa John, pizza magnate, as a gift to the public to reflect his love of the outdoors. His creation consists of a multiple-use trail along a beautiful stream valley, over impressive stone bridges, through wildflower meadows, across wetland boardwalks, and along a lovely lake. This is a great walk in any season. In the spring you will enjoy the wildflowers, summer will feature planted flower and vegetable gardens, and in the fall, there will be pumpkin patches in addition to the abundance of natural features. Winter is a great time to visit also, as the landscape was designed with the cross-country ski trails of Colorado in mind. It's a beautiful walk any time of the year. There are nature trails that cut across the main paved trail if you care to venture a little more into the natural areas.

For a treat after your walk, we suggest the Homemade Ice Cream and Pie Kitchen in Middletown, about two miles away. To get there, turn left on Evergreen Road, then left on Shelbyville Road. The Pie Kitchen is at 12531 Shelbyville Road.

BROWN AND ARTHUR K. DRAUT PARKS

JEFFERSON COUNTY, KENTUCKY

Walking Path: Each park offers paved walks of about one mile. Completely accessible.

Features: Brown Park paths traverse woodlands and stream areas; Arthur K. Draut Park offers scenic wetland boardwalks.

Facilities: Portable restroom at Brown Park near the playground and picnic shelter.

Getting there: Brown Park is located on Kresge Way at Browns Lane in St. Matthews. Arthur K. Draut Park is located on Bowling Boulevard (Kresge turns into Bowling going east). There is a sidewalk connecting the two parks along Bowling Boulevard.

www.stmatthews.org

Brown Park is a nature walker's oasis in the middle of suburbia. It features beautiful winding paved walkways that snake through acres of scenery including thick woods, bridges and Beargrass Creek. Be sure to crisscross your walk through the center of the park instead of simply looping around the outskirts. All directions are rewarding. At the back of the park is an old graveyard surrounded by a high brick wall.

For a longer walk, head out of Brown Park across Kresge Way east to Bowling Boulevard and pick up the walking path to Arthur K. Draut Park. Alternatively, drive from Brown to Draut Park; there is a small parking area on Bowling Boulevard.

Arthur K. Draut Park offers a walking path with creek-crossing bridges, stone benches, and dedicated wetlands. It is another hidden park gem—one must get out of the car and walk the paths to see and experience the natural area. It is a very rewarding short walk, so don't miss it.

A nice long walk through both of these lovely St. Matthews parks deserves an ice cream treat. We suggest Chillers at 4123 Shelbyville Road. From Brown Park, cross Kresge, and turn right on South Hubbards Lane. Drive about one mile and turn left on Shelbyville Road. Chillers is on the right at Thierman Lane.

BUFFALO TRACE PARK

HARRISON COUNTY, INDIANA

Walking Path: 1.3 miles, paved and accessible.

Features: Rustic lake and woodland walk.

Facilities: Restroom buildings at pool house and camp ground.

Getting there: I64 W to Exit 119- US 150/Greenville. Drive west approximately 15 miles. Park is on the right. Watch for park sign – easy to miss! During the summer season, there is a $5-per-car charge for non-Harrison County residents.

www.harrisoncoparks.com

This rural recreational park offers a 30-acre lake as its centerpiece. During the summer season, the park also offers swimming, fishing, paddleboat rental, a petting zoo, and camping. The 1.3-mile walking path circumnavigates the beautiful lake. This park makes a nice outing during any season. We especially love the lake walk in the winter, when you will likely view hundreds of geese and waterfowl wintering along the lake. Several winter visits, we were treated to the sight of many geese flying in for a slippery landing on the semi-frozen lake. Children will especially like the antics of the birds as they slip and slide on the ice. The walking path loops up through the wooded camping area a bit; if you are lucky, there will be the woodsy smell of campfires in the air. Benches are placed along the lake to sit and enjoy the expansive view. Check the park website for when Santa is scheduled to visit, and you may enjoy a hot chocolate at the park after your walk.

One of our favorite places to get a bite and a treat after visiting Buffalo Trace is Pal's Diner, located just up US 150 in Palmyra, less than a mile away. Alas, at this writing, the diner was closed for remodeling. We hope they reopen soon! If a drive through tiny Palmyra after your visit turns up no ice cream, your best bet is to head back toward I-64 on US 150 and hit the Dairy Queen for a blizzard on your way home. There is also a local coffee shop: Bean Street Coffee Company, located across from the Dairy Queen on US 150.

CHEROKEE PARK–BARINGER HILL PATH

JEFFERSON COUNTY, KENTUCKY

Walking Path: One mile, paved.

Features: Paved wooded walk with bridges over creek.

Facilities: Located at the top of Baringer Hill

Getting there: Enter Cherokee Park off Lexington Road at Cochran Hill Road. Turn right at the Scenic Loop and park along the road. The entrance to the trail is across the roadway. Look for the Baringer Hill Path sign.

http://louisvilleky.gov/government/parks/park-list/cherokee-park

This lovely park walking path branches off in two directions. One will take you along the meadow at the base of Baringer Hill; the other follows along the creek and over wooden bridges then descends to Baringer Spring. Walk as far as you like, then backtrack and go the other direction before heading back to your car. This is a great summer evening walk along the stream, plus deep shade and the coolness of the stone Baringer spring area.

To cool off after your walk, treat yourself at the Homemade Pie and Ice Cream Kitchen located at 1041 Bardstown Road, a few miles away. Continue on the Scenic Loop to the next right and exit back to Lexington Road. Turn left and drive to Grinstead Drive. Turn left at Grinstead and then turn right on Bardstown Road. The Pie Kitchen is on the right.

IROQUOIS PARK

JEFFERSON COUNTY, KENTUCKY

Walking Path: 1.6 miles, paved; somewhat rough in spots but mostly accessible with caution.

Features: Classic Olmsted park landscapes, stately old-growth trees, state-of-the-art accessible playground.

Facilities: Restroom building located at the playground.

Getting there: Off Taylor Boulevard/New Cut Road at Southern Parkway or Kenwood Drive.

http://louisvilleky.gov/government/parks/park-list/iroquois-park

Iroquois Park was planned by Frederick Law Olmsted as a "scenic reservation" of forested hillsides and breathtaking vistas. The park features the WPA-era Iroquois Amphitheater, an open-air theater that accommodates 2,366 people. This walk will allow you to experience the natural scenery, woodlands, and beautiful landscapes that are the hallmark of an Olmsted park.

Enter the park at the second entrance off New Cut Road at Kenwood Drive—the amphitheater entrance—and park near the play area. Look for the paved walkway along New Cut Road. The path makes a loop up toward the first park entrance at Taylor Boulevard and then returns. It is a multi-use path appropriate for strollers and wheelchairs. It may be a bit bumpy in places and contain tree debris, so be careful. If you have children with you, be sure to plan time to visit the state-of-the-art, accessible play area appropriate for children with physical disabilities.

This walk is restful and restorative as you meander along the open meadows and huge old-growth trees. If you are up for a nature trail, cross the road at the Taylor Boulevard entrance and pick up a woodland nature trail to wander into the forested hillside a bit. You'll find your way back to the play area or the amphitheater easily.

There is a Dairy Queen a few miles away at 4137 Taylor Boulevard toward I-264 if you want an ice cream treat after your visit.

SAM PEDEN COMMUNITY PARK

FLOYD COUNTY, INDIANA

Walking Path: 1.25 miles, paved multi-use, and accessible.

Features: Walk around a nice-sized lake and woodlands.

Facilities: Restroom buildings near playground.

Getting there: I64 W/St. Louis. Take Exit 121 to I265. Exit 3 to Grantline Road/IN 111. Drive one mile; park is on the right.

http://www.floydcountyparks.org

Sam Peden Community Park offers varied recreation opportunities for the people of New Albany and Floyd County, including fishing, volleyball, tennis and basketball courts, horseshoe pits, picnic shelters, woodland nature trails, and a paved walking path. People come from all over Floyd County and beyond to enjoy this pretty park in the heart of suburban New Albany. The paved path winds all the way around the lake making for a nice challenging walk. Kids will enjoy the park's fields, the big lake, and play areas.

A summer excursion is nice; ice cream is available back up Grantline Road toward I-264 at the Dairy Queen. A local soft-serve favorite, Mom and Pop's Cone Corner, operated in the opposite direction on Grantline Road for many years. At the time of this writing, the family has closed the outlet. We can only hope they will decide to reopen in the future.

SENECA PARK

JEFFERSON COUNTY, KENTUCKY

Walking Path: 1.2 miles, paved.

Features: Olmstead parklands, stately trees, winding path.

Facilities: Restroom building at playground along path.

Getting there: Cannons Lane at Pee Wee Reese Road or Rock Creek Drive. Parking along Pee Wee Reese Road or in parking area on Rock Creek Drive.

http://louisvilleky.gov/government/parks/park-list/seneca-park

The walking option at Seneca Park we highlight here for you is the 1.2-mile paved walking path that circles the sports fields, tennis courts, and playground. I have to admit that in my younger days I was a bit of a snob about not including this walk as an option for a true nature outing. In fact, I shunned it completely in our last book, *Take A Hike, Louisville!* (we covered a more adventurous outing along the cross-country trail in that book). My reasoning was that the paved path didn't have a standout nature feature, which was a prerequisite for inclusion in our previous book.

I have now realized that I did not truly appreciate what this path offers: a stroll through a lovely Olmstead Park along a gently winding path, surrounded by beautiful landscapes and stately trees. I think in my younger days I spent so much time at this park pushing a stroller quickly around the sports fields, anxious for the stroller occupant's sibling to finish practice on those sports fields so that we could get on the long road home, that I just never saw the forest for the trees, so to speak.

Return visits to Seneca Park in later years have allowed us to walk more slowly with an appreciation of the beautiful surroundings. And really, how could one go wrong in an Olmstead park, anyway?

So go ahead and take this leisurely 1.2-mile stroll along a relatively level and mostly shaded paved path. Any time of the day in any season will be very nice. I have walked in the early mornings here, enjoying the layers of fog that sometimes form and drift out in the fields. Afternoons will provide the sounds of rambunctious youth at practice or younger children's laughter lifting on the breezes as they play on the playground—both music to my older ears. An evening walk is good here too, as there are always folks running, walking, or jogging into the night. You will never be alone out on this trail. If solitude is what you are looking for, this is not the walk for you; but if happy, active people cheer you up, take this walk soon.

For an ice cream treat after your walk, if you are so inclined, check out Graeter's in St. Matthews. Go across Cannons Lane from Pee Wee Reese Road and up about seven blocks on Willis Avenue. Turn right on Breckenridge Lane. Graeter's is at 140 Breckenridge Lane.

THURMAN HUTCHINS PARK

JEFFERSON COUNTY, KENTUCKY

Walking Path: About 1.5 miles, paved and accessible.

Features: Lake and pier.

Facilities: Restroom building located near playground and sports fields.

Getting there: I-71 to Zorn Avenue N, east on River Road. Park is on the right.

http://louisvilleky.gov/government/parks/park-list/ thurman-hutchins-park

Thurman Hutchins Park is located along River Road across from the better-known Carrie Gaulbert Cox Park, which is a picnicking mecca. Thurman Hutchins Park is recognized more for its soccer and baseball fields, but the walk around the lake, short boardwalk trails across wetlands, and another half-mile walk east on River Road to the Patriots Peace Memorial make this a nice walking excursion.

Your walk will probably take you around a few fishermen—it's popular here, and the pier is nice for this activity, as well as simply observing the lake and fish swimming below. It's quiet and restful. Stretch your legs a bit further with a visit to the Patriots Peace Memorial up River Road about a quarter mile, and plan to spend a little time enjoying the serenity inside the memorial and beside the reflecting pool.

For ice cream after stretching those legs, we suggest heading back up Zorn Avenue, across Brownsboro Road (Zorn turns into Hillcrest Avenue) to Frankfort Avenue and turn right. Drive 1.1 miles and find Comfy Cow on your right. We think Comfy Cow is Louisville's best local ice cream shop. Yum!

THE KOESTERS FAMILY

Lucynda Koesters met her husband, Willi, in the 1980s when they both worked for a Louisville advertising agency. They spent much time in nature in their early years hiking and camping together. Children, careers, and sports intervened in the middle years, making it harder to find time for outdoor excursions, but the love of nature had taken hold.

Now, with two adult children and a preteen, the family makes it a priority once again to get out and enjoy nature walks whenever possible. Willi and Lucynda's first book together, *Take A Hike, Louisville!*, published by Butler Books in 2009, was a family project and local favorite.

Take A Walk, Louisville! is their answer to the challenges of outdoor adventures as one ages, has small children in tow, or is caregiving for an elderly or able-challenged person.

Lucynda is currently the director of Nutrition and Senior Centers for LifeSpan Resources, Inc., the Area Agency on Aging for Clark, Floyd, Harrison, and Scott Counties, Indiana. Willi is enjoying his "encore" career as an engineering technician at Amatrol, Inc., in Jeffersonville, Indiana. His photography these days is of his personal favorite work: nature, landscapes, and family.

Gracie, the Koesters' youngest child, and constant hiking and walking companion, is now a preteen. She loves school, reading, art, and taking nature walks with Mom and Dad. She walked all but one of the walks in this book. The family feels truly blessed.

Willi, Lucy and Gracie enjoying an ice cream treat at
Comfy Cow in New Albany after their walk.